UNLEASHING *the* TEACHER *in* YOU!

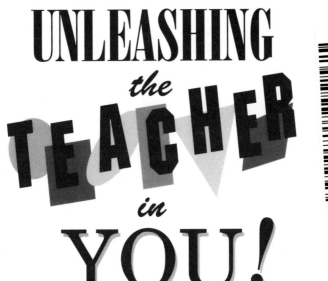

Teaching the Bible So Your Students Will Learn

WESLEY R. WILLIS

ACCENT PUBLICATIONS
Denver, Colorado

Accent Publications
12100 West Sixth Avenue
P.O. Box 15337
Denver, Colorado 80215

Copyright © 1992 Accent Publications
Printed in the United States of America

Library of Congress Catalog Card Number 92-71709

ISBN 0-89636-285-X

CONTENTS

INTRODUCTION

All of us have been taught by many different teachers. And these instructors have exerted a powerful influence in our lives.

Perhaps the teachers who made the greatest impact were those who taught us when we were very young. These teachers include parents, brothers and sisters, other relatives, friends, and leaders in church programs. Except for our relatives, we may very well have forgotten the names of these teachers. In most of our early learning experiences, we didn't even recognize that we were receiving instruction. These lessons came as a natural part of living.

But we did learn. And what we learned from those teachers has continued to influence how we think, feel, and act. Recently, I was talking to a young man who has experienced great academic success. He shared with me that much of his motivation to excel was triggered by a junior high school math teacher. Up until that time this young man had drifted along in school. His grades were acceptable, but not outstanding. However, when he encountered this teacher, he was forced into serious reevaluation. From that course on, all the way through high school, this young man never

5

earned anything less than an A. He subsequently excelled both in college and graduate school. And he attributes his motivation for excellence to a junior high math teacher.

What could cause a teacher to have such an impact in a young person's life? Probably two things. This excellent teacher challenges her students through her approach to teaching. She is well-prepared, employs effective methods, and triggers her students' internal motivation through challenge and freedom. She treats them as competent, intelligent individuals; they respond appropriately. She understands and practices excellent teaching.

But beyond her approach to teaching, this excellent teacher influences her students by who she is. She is a loving, godly, concerned teacher. And in addition to teaching math concepts to her students, she shares herself also. This teacher is interested in her students as people, not just math learners. When excellent teaching methods combine with a deep, genuine concern for students, those students find it extremely difficult not to learn.

Our prayer is that this book will help you think through what you are doing to influence your students—and how you are doing it. But beyond that, we hope each teacher will recognize that teaching is more than methods and materials. Teaching grows out of what we are even more than what we do.

As you read through this book, recognize that the Bible studies and other exercises are an integral part. Don't just scan them; work through each question. You will discover important truths from the Bible, and you also will think through your approach to teaching.

Most chapters in this book contain portions that have appeared in periodical publications. Part of chapter one was published in *Discipleship Journal*. Portions of chapters two through six appeared in the *Sunday School Planner*. Part of chapter seven was published in *Christian Education Today*. And part of chapter nine appeared in *Action*.

Leading with a
Servant's Heart

Some years ago two brothers were born into a family where they learned the meaning of hard work. Their father owned his own business, and from their earliest recollection, Johnny and Jim had worked with him. They knew what it was like to reach the end of the day stiff, sore, and exhausted—too tired to sleep.

Johnny, the more sensitive of the two, and his brother Jim both were outdoorsmen who reveled in their physical strength. This strength, coupled with short fuses and violent behavior often created problems for the brothers. Consequently, as the boys grew up, they were known as the "terrors of the neighborhood."

But they were good workers and, as the years wore on, their father increasingly relied on Johnny and Jim to help him run the business. Because of their faithfulness, their dad willingly entrusted them with the family net assets.

When they left, their father was shocked.

Just as Johnny and Jim were finishing up a major project with their father, they abandoned him. He had planned to hand the business over to his sons—to let them take what he had built and expand it from there. But these two sons turned their back on all of that and left their father to fend for himself as best he could.

The situation arose when the boys saw the chance to hit it big. They knew they might never get another opportunity like this, and they just couldn't pass it up. A young leader, putting together a new organization, arrived in town and handpicked a select few to work with him in a special venture. When he invited Johnny and Jim to join his elite group, they readily abandoned their father. They turned their back on their commitment, their plans, and all of their father's dreams to jump at the chance of a lifetime.

But there were many things Johnny and Jim had not anticipated. They operated on a different schedule from their boss, and they viewed life very differently. He was patient and methodical; they were anxious and impetuous. He believed in serving people; they wanted to use them. But even worse, they hadn't considered the implications of being little fish in a big pond. In the family business, they were right next to the man in charge—no jockeying, no power plays, no pecking order. But once the brothers "signed on the dotted line," they were just two more members of the executive team. And soon it became apparent that others on that team were smarter or more aggressive.

So Johnny and Jim conspired to get an edge on the others by seeking an opportune time to talk their boss into reorganizing in order to maneuver themselves into positions of prominence. The opportunity came on a business trip. Johnny and Jim got their boss off by himself and suggested that when he was ready to establish his formal organization, they could become his right-hand and left-hand men. Perhaps one could be Chief Executive Officer and the other Chief Operating Officer. And just in case their suggestions weren't enough, they arranged for a close relative to plead the case with their boss.

But their plot could not be concealed for long. When the news leaked out, the brothers were ostracized immediately. Their peers (and erstwhile friends) began plotting counter-moves to block the brothers, and to protect their own rights.

Naturally the boss caught rumors of unrest and insurrection, and immediately called an executive committee meeting. With great sorrow he informed them that they had totally missed the purpose of the training sessions he had conducted so carefully. He explained that his organization was built on giving not getting—on service rather than privilege. The only way to get ahead was to promote others rather than self. The one who pushed and promoted himself would always wind up last, whereas the one who served others willingly would occupy the place of honor. It was a hard lesson to learn because it ran so counter to the prevailing culture.

Perhaps you've heard the saying, "the more things change, the more they stay the same." Although these events actually took place almost twenty centuries ago in the life and ministry of

Jesus, the principles are totally relevant today. They certainly run counter to contemporary prescriptions of dressing for success, winning through intimidation, taking care of "number one." James and John, the sons of thunder, had to learn that those who would follow Christ must live according to the values and principles of their Leader.

And His guidelines haven't changed. As followers of Christ, we are called to serve. He expects us to look for ways to promote and elevate others rather than to fight, scratch, and claw for our own rights. The biblical principle is clear. "...Whosoever will be great among you, shall be your minister: and whosoever of you will be the chiefest, shall be the servant of all. For even the Son of man came not to be ministered unto, but to minister, and to give his life a ransom for many" (Mark 10:43-45).

Clear? Yes. But understandable? Probably not. And the concept certainly violates natural human nature. All of our human drives and desires scream out, contradicting the principle of winning through losing—of getting to the top by heading for the bottom—of coming in first by trying to be last. Our human nature tells us, "Stand up for your rights; use whatever clout you have to get an edge. If you don't look out for 'number one' who else will?"

Teaching or assisting in some aspect of a Christian education program offers excellent servant leadership opportunities. Servant leadership requires no sophisticated training or particular skills. We don't have to go overseas or raise support money. What it does require is a willingness to obey Christ and to allow His Spirit to serve others through us. And we can demonstrate such leadership as we prepare to teach, as we interact in class with students, and as we spend time with them outside of class.

I have a friend who chairs a department in a graduate school. In addition to his earned doctorate, he has many other credentials and is recognized worldwide. He loves his discipline and thoroughly enjoys the challenges of helping to expand understanding and to trigger the insight of eager graduate students. But if you want to see him really excited, ask about the junior boys' Sunday School class he teaches. He is more enthusiastic about one pre-teen boy who makes a spiritual commitment than about the praise of scholars who are impressed with his wisdom.

Several years ago I was asked by a group of Christian educators in India to conduct a series of Christian Education seminars. Naturally I sent them my biographical information as part of our preparation. Wherever I went, my hosts used information from my *vita*. It was interesting to me that one specific thing always was mentioned— whether meeting with publishers, academics, or church leaders. As different persons introduced me, invariably they included the fact that I taught a sixth grade boys' Sunday School class.

My professor friend and I have had similar experiences. People are moderately interested in credentials. They are polite when you tell where

13

you earned your doctorate. Some even stifle boredom enough to ask the topic of your dissertation. But the bottom line is, "Can you serve?" And people know that you do serve when teaching a Sunday School class is high on your priority list. (You don't teach Junior boys for glory and prestige.)

God has not given everyone the gift of teaching—He calls us to a wide variety of ministries. But wherever you assist, if you love your students, giving your time to help them grow and mature is one way to follow Jesus' teaching and serve them.

Of course, servant leadership can apply to other areas of life beyond church ministry. What about co-workers where we are employed? We can serve them, too. Most of us have stereotyped images of business executives who wield great power ruthlessly. We think of an executive moving into a failing automobile company and, through personal power and charisma, dramatically turning it around (so the autobiography claims). Or perhaps we read of corporate raiders who determine the fate of major corporations and thousands of workers as nonchalantly as we choose our brand of toothpaste.

But that's not what corporate life is all about. The true leaders—the ones who lead not drive—are the leaders who serve those reporting to them. These are the effective leaders. And these are the executives who are able to serve God through the routine of corporate life.

Recently, a young lady related her experience of working for a leader who served her. She had been sent on a business trip—one of her first—to the west coast. Since she travelled alone infrequently, she left with some anxiety. Neither she nor one of the executives realized that they had been scheduled on the same flight, and both were surprised when they met near the baggage claim area. Even though the executive had his luggage, he waited for hers to arrive and helped her with it.

Then came the rental car. They both were renting from the same company, but there had been some mix-up on her reservation. Although the executive already had his assigned car, he waited and attempted to help clear up the confusion. He finally solved the problem by charging her car to his account. And when she finally received her car, he went out of his way to lead her through city traffic to her motel. After helping carry her luggage to her room, he went on to his own hotel to prepare for his meetings.

Later, this young lady related to me that she had observed servant leadership in action. Although it was inconvenient, the executive chose to give his time to help a co-worker several rungs below him on the corporate ladder. By serving her, he became an excellent leader to her. And an additional fringe benefit is loyalty and appreciation that even a salary raise could not buy.

Professors and executives who cook hamburgers for the High School youth group serve God while serving the teens. Women who share their love in a noisy infant nursery, although they prefer participating in the adult meeting, serve by emulating Christ's attitude, "Permit the children to come to Me...." (Luke 18:16, NASB). Corporate leaders working in children's church do not stoop beneath their dignity, but minister as servant leaders. And private intercessory prayer, asking God to bless another's efforts, is a private demonstration of a servant's heart. Washing church linens, maintaining attendance records, counting the offering, setting up chairs, and countless other jobs comprise the indispensable "behind the scenes" servant corps.

Among believers today, much attention is given to the subject of developing our spiritual gifts. People flock to the seminars of those who have the latest word about this Christian topic. We encourage Christians to learn how to share their faith and then challenge them with the importance of discipling others after salvation. But it is possible to do all of these very good things with improper motivation. Teaching, preaching, writing, and leading others can be a euphoric trip into the rarified atmosphere of public acclaim.

On the other hand, teaching children in Sunday School is grunt work. It isn't glamorous and there's precious little public acclaim. But if we are concerned about power and position and the perks that come to leaders, we are no different from the pagans who also seek such things. We live as lords of the Gentiles.

When His disciples tried their power play, Jesus reminded them that they were to operate by a set of guidelines different from those who were spiritually blind. Unfortunately, some contemporary Christian leaders seem to follow the guidelines that Jesus said characterized the Gentiles. Whether we serve as leaders in key positions or as subordinates with little acclaim, we all are called to serve. Jesus instructs us, His disciples in this day, "...whosoever will be great among you, let him be your minister; and whosoever will be chief among you, let him be your servant" (Matthew 20:26-27).

God expects us to copy the leadership style of Jesus. He gave Himself a ransom for us, so that we could become all that He is and all that He has planned for us to become. Many people placed demands on Jesus, but He always chose to do what was best for them. He served them rather than doing what was easiest or most convenient for Himself, and this attitude is what He expects of His followers in every age.

In the upper room, after Jesus washed the disciples' feet, He explained, "For I have given you an example, that ye should do as I have done to you. Verily, verily, I say unto you, The servant is not greater than his lord, neither he that is sent greater than he that sent him" (John 13:15-16). In the kingdom of God, greatness comes through service and humility. As we promote and encourage others, we grow and mature in Christ-likeness.

CONSIDER GOD'S WORD

Although some of the details included about the early life of James and John (Johnny and Jim) are speculative, the ideas are based on the scriptural account. The passages dealing with the call and early life of James and John include Mark 1:19-20, 3:17; Matthew 4:21-22. Let's consider in more detail Jesus' teaching about servant leadership recorded in Mark 10:35-45 and Matthew 20:20-28. Although the accounts are similar, notice the variations. They do not contradict each other, but neither gives all of the details.

Read *Matthew 20:20-28 and Mark 10:35-45*. How does the phrase "with her sons" (Matthew 20:20-21) give us a clue as to how James and John could ask Jesus (Mark 10:35) and at the same time Matthew could have written that their mother asked Him?

Mark 10:35. Notice how James and John (along with their mother) came to Jesus. They probably came in the same way that they often had come to their parents (as many children do), trying to get Jesus to agree to do something before telling Him what they wanted done. What was their request?

Mark 10:37. Compare the other disciples' response in Mark 10:41 with the brothers' request in verse 37. What do you think the other disciples thought that James and John were asking Jesus to do for them?

Why do you think the other disciples responded so negatively?

Mark 10:37-39. In light of Mark 10:32-33, what do you think Jesus meant when He asked the brothers if they could drink His cup and share His baptism?

19

Read *Luke 18:31-34*, especially verse 34.
The brothers did not understand what Jesus
meant. What do you think they assumed He
was talking about?

How would Jesus' promise to the brothers
(Mark 10:39) ultimately be fulfilled?

Mark 10:41-45. These verses contain Jesus'
teaching about His style of leadership compared to
the way the "lords of the Gentiles" (ungodly
leaders) led their followers. On the chart that
follows, list the characteristics of the Servant
Leaders and the Ungodly Leaders.

SERVANT LEADERS   UNGODLY LEADERS

Which style of leadership have you seen demonstrated most often?

What can you do to change your style of leadership to be more like what Jesus wanted His followers to practice?

Mark 10:41 (compare ***Matthew 20:24).*** What were the consequences when the brothers followed the ungodly style of leadership?

How do you and others you know respond to the ungodly style of leadership today?

Mark 10:45 (also compare *John 13:2-17).* How did Jesus demonstrate appropriate leadership when He was on earth?

And how did people respond to Jesus' style of leadership? (Compare John 1:35-51, 3:1-21, 6:63-69, 8:38-59, 10:22-42.)

John 13:17. What consequences can we expect if we lead as Jesus led?

CONSIDER YOUR MINISTRY

All of us who are responsible for others serve in a leadership capacity. Pastors give guidance to all church members and especially to associates and lay leaders within the congregation. Sunday School superintendents lead departmental superintendents and teachers. And teachers of individual classes lead and give guidance to their students. Whenever we have the privilege of ministering, we function in a leadership role.

1. List those whom you are responsible to lead.

In what ways do they look to you for guidance or help?

2. How might you act toward them if you were leading in the way that Jesus described as acting like the lords of the Gentiles?

How do you think that those whom you lead might respond if you were to lead them in this way?

23

Why do you think that they would respond in this way?

3. How would those same persons respond if you were to lead them as Jesus led His followers—as a servant leader?

Why would they respond in this manner?

4. What personality traits, attitudes, actions, situations might hinder you from leading as a servant leader?

Write out a brief prayer in which you express to God your desire for how you would like to lead as a servant leader. Confess those things that hinder you from following through on this commitment and ask Him to help you be faithful as a servant leader.

2

Loving the Little Rascals

Teachers whom I meet at seminars and conventions regularly ask for suggestions to help them in teaching. One of the most common problems that teachers mention is handling discipline—how to control their students. The questions are asked in various ways, but the meaning is usually the same.

"Can you give any suggestions for maintaining control in my class?"

Sometimes the question takes the form of a statement.

"It seems as though students really don't have any respect for the Bible nowadays."

But others just explode with frustration.

"The little rascals are driving me out of my mind!"

Whatever way it is phrased, teachers usually state the symptom—they don't address the real problem. It may be true that the teacher struggles with controlling student behavior, but the crucial question is *"why?"* *Why* is there a problem with control? *What* is causing the symptomatic unruly behavior?

Several summers ago I experienced severe pain

in my left leg. After an examination and X-rays, the doctor concluded that my leg was not the source of the problem. The real problem was in my back; the leg pain was a symptom. Torn ligaments in my back caused inflammation and muscle tension that put pressure on my sciatic nerve. Hence, pain in my leg.

Likewise, discipline problems in the Sunday School (the symptom) may stem from a variety of sources (the real problem). Some students come from homes with an extremely high confusion tolerance. The parents of these children may be able to maintain their sanity and still allow their offspring substantial freedom. To those of us with a low confusion threshold, such a possibility seems inconceivable. But some temperaments seem to thrive in a relaxed, hang-loose atmosphere rather than a regulated, disciplined household.

Another source of undisciplined students is parents at the opposite end of the control spectrum—overly strict parents. Research studies have shown that, in the long run, harsh discipline is worse for children than loose discipline. It is difficult to be very strict with children consistently, and consistency is crucial in child-rearing.

Recently, in the course of a weekend, I observed two parents who were very strict with their early elementary age children. Although these parents enforced strict discipline in most areas, there were some areas that the parents didn't have the energy to enforce. Even if such parents are consistently strict in all areas, they cannot exert control when they are not around. Which is why a child who is rigidly controlled at home often goes wild as soon as he gets away from his parents.

There also is the possibility that the parents of some unruly children we teach dislike noise and confusion, but have no idea how to stop it. Or, in some rare cases, perhaps the parents really don't care enough for their children to be willing to guide, supervise, and even discipline when appropriate (Proverbs 3:12, 13:24).

But whether the parents prefer loose discipline or are harsh and demanding, whether they don't know how to direct their children or don't care, the result is the same in your classroom—confusion and frustration for the teacher, turmoil in the class. It takes little insight to recognize that while one undisciplined child alone may be tolerable, if you have a class full, the result is chaos. Explaining the problem to the parents and soliciting their support may help some, but that is only a partial solution. You, the teacher in the classroom, have to deal with the problem.

Unfortunately, many elementary and secondary school teachers also struggle to resolve the same problem. Teachers and administrators must cope with the consequences of children growing up in a society with fewer and fewer restraints. Some school and classroom policies compound the problem. And school teachers who do not command respect, or who cannot manage their students, add to an already serious situation.

In spite of all these obstacles, there are many teachers doing an excellent job in a wide variety of local church ministries. And it is not necessarily because the parents are outstanding disciplinarians or because their school system is highly structured.

Excellent teachers have learned a vital truth about disciplining their classes. You can't wait until you have a problem to discipline. These teachers give regular guidance to students and thereby head off problems "at the pass."

Perhaps the single greatest barrier to effective class control is thinking of discipline as reactive—a response to a problem. However, truly effective discipline occurs when students' energy is channeled into productive areas so that problems do not arise.

We can glean much from God's exhortation for parents: "...bring them up in the nurture and admonition of the Lord" (Ephesians 6:4). The word "nurture" could be translated as "discipline." But it is important that we understand a biblical definition of "nurture."

The Bible Knowledge Commentary states the meaning of nurture as "...'child discipline', including directing and correcting; cf. 'training' in righteousness (II Timothy 3:16) and God's 'discipline of believers' (Hebrews 12:8)." True discipline does not necessarily mean punishment or even control. Those who discipline most effectively give guidance and direction.

When parents and teachers offer such guidance and direction, most of what we consider discipline problems disappear. Let's look at some suggestions for preventing problems in class rather than waiting until after they arise to deal with them.

PREPARE WELL. There is no substitute for a well-prepared teacher. From my observations, control could improve dramatically in most classes through more effective preparation. For some teachers this means spending more time preparing to teach or beginning earlier in the week. Or, if you are spending adequate time, it may mean utilizing the time you are spending more productively. Many teachers find that they prepare much more effectively when they meticulously follow the preparation suggestions in the Teacher's Guide. Another strategy is to approach the best teacher in your church and ask how he or she prepares. This can provide valuable insight to aid in your own preparation.

KNOW YOUR STUDENTS PERSONALLY. The teacher who has built a personal relationship with students rarely has to worry much about controlling those students. This inevitably requires spending time with students outside of class. Inviting them into your home, having a soft drink after school, attending their sporting events, and planning outings with them—these are some good ways to get to know them. You really don't know your students until you can call them by name without thinking. You also should know the names of other family members and what special topics of conversation are unique to each individual student you teach.

PLAN MEANINGFUL CLASSES. Once you get to know your students personally, it is far easier to plan lessons that speak to their needs. As curriculum writers and editors prepare lesson materials, they try to suggest relevant class activities and illustrations. But you must personalize these suggestions. You know your students' real needs and can tailor class activities and class sessions to speak directly and effectively to those needs. When your lesson addresses those areas where your students are hurting, you rarely have to cope with control problems.

GET STUDENTS ACTIVELY INVOLVED. Good teachers know that they cannot entertain their students. No matter how hard you work to plan interesting and exciting lectures, most students will become bored if you do all the talking. It is normal for people to become excited about what they do, and less excited about what others are doing. Our students are no different. When class activities get students involved in participative learning, their enthusiasm for that class increases. This means planning meaningful projects. It means using discussion and question-answer techniques. It means recognizing that the worthwhile things happening in class are those things that involve the students. Our job as teachers is to make sure that the right things happen in class. Then true learning can occur.

CHALLENGE ACTIVE MINDS. One highly effective teaching strategy is to enable students to discover truth for themselves. This approach to teaching encourages students to dig into the Word of God to find out what God has said. But in order to adopt such an approach, we need to forsake the notion that a teacher's sole job is to dispense knowledge. What a teacher really needs to do is make sure that learning takes place. When students discover truth for themselves, they become far more excited than when we tell them what God says. As you teach, try to stimulate questions in students' minds. Encourage them to ask those questions. Then help them to find the answers. In this way you will cultivate a desire to learn and students who become independent learners. In the final analysis, that is the very best teaching that any of us can do.

Now I would love to be able to assure you that if you follow all of these suggestions you will never have class control problems. Unfortunately, I can't. Occasionally, some of your students may become rowdy and disruptive. But I do guarantee that applying proactive discipline will help to minimize such problems. But, no matter how proactive a teacher becomes, reactive discipline will be necessary at times. And although it is not enjoyable to administer, there is significant personal value that comes from disciplining our students. In fact, God uses discipline in each of our lives to help produce the fruit of righteousness. It is important for us to recognize that compassionately administered discipline is an expression of love.

Our teaching goal ought to be proactive discipline—dealing with our students in such a way that we avoid having to punish them. But in some cases we will have to respond to students' wrong behavior or improper attitudes. And when we do need to rebuke or otherwise enforce discipline, it always should be for the welfare of the student, not for the teacher's catharsis. Sometimes a frown of disapproval in class or a gentle verbal rebuke after class is enough. At other times a teacher might need to refer the problem to a superintendent or meet with a child's parents. Sometimes you might even need to dismiss a student from class or not allow one to participate in special events. But even when such extreme measures are taken, *a positive, kind spirit* will make the discipline far more effective.

Recognize that even the unpleasant experiences can have lasting benefit for the students. And whether you discipline your students proactively or reactively, you will be contributing to their long-term growth. And you really will be able to love those "little rascals."

CONSIDER GOD'S WORD

It is unfortunate that whenever we use the word "discipline," many people think of "punishment." Biblical discipline embodies a far broader concept than punishment. Because Jesus has taken the eternal punishment for our sins, we will not suffer the ultimate punishment of separation from God for eternity. But in this life, God still disciplines us. He disciplines us as children, not for the purpose of preventing banishment from His family, but to help us develop godly qualities in our lives. Sometimes God's discipline is reactive, helping us to change behavior. But He also uses discipline to help us develop godliness. Just as an athlete disciplines himself to build strength and endurance, God's proactive discipline nurtures our spiritual strength and endurance.

Several key passages describe the discipline that comes to us from God. Perhaps the most comprehensive of these is Hebrews 12:3-11. Read through this passage and notice all of the references to discipline or chastening. None of these refer to eternal punishment. Rather, they describe God's proactive dealing with us here and now. This passage begins by recounting some of the experiences that Jesus had when He was living and ministering here on earth.

Hebrews 12:3-4. How much did Jesus suffer?

Who caused His suffering?

Why is this important to you?

As you face suffering, how can you find comfort in the suffering of Jesus?

Hebrews 12:5-8. These verses present us with options of how we might respond when God disciplines us through circumstances that He brings into our lives.

> *Verse 5.* What two inappropriate responses might we have when we are chastened (disciplined) by God?

> *Verse 6.* What are the two very important truths that chastening from God helps us to understand?

> *Verse 7.* What else does God's chastening teach us?

Verse 8. And what would it indicate to us if we didn't receive any chastening from God?

Hebrews 12:9-10. The writer of the book of Hebrews compares God and our earthly fathers in order to help us understand how we should respond when we experience chastening from God.

Verse 9. What is the normal response to loving discipline from earthly fathers?

How does this concept relate to the way we ought to respond to God?

Verse 10. What is the difference between the way an earthly father chastens us and how God chastens us?

Hebrews 12:11. What is the short-term response to chastening?

In contrast to the short-term response, what long-term benefit can we receive?

Try to think of a time when you experienced circumstances that may have been used by God to help you mature. What were the circumstances surrounding that experience?

How did you feel during the experience?

How do you feel now as you look back on it?

How did the experience contribute to your growth and maturity? Did it yield "the peaceable fruit of righteousness" (Hebrew 12:11)?

CONSIDER YOUR MINISTRY

We who teach do our students a disservice when we allow them to behave in a rude or unruly manner. We need to help them learn what is proper behavior, especially as they grow and mature in Christ. But as we look at poor behavior, we need to examine the way we prepare and teach the Bible. If we have not done *our* homework, we really cannot be too harsh to students who exhibit inappropriate behavior.

And if we have prepared well, so that we know the lesson that we intend to teach, we need to consider the methods we use. Are they appropriate to the class?

Finally, we need to make sure that we hold our students accountable for their behavior after we have done all that we can do.

Evaluate yourself.

1. How much time do you usually spend in preparing your lesson?

A good rule of thumb is to spend no less than four times the length of your teaching time in preparation. That is, if you have 30 minutes of teaching time, plan to spend no less than two hours in preparation. If the material is unfamiliar or difficult, you will want to spend more time.

> Based on the length of your lesson time, what is the minimum time you should spend in study and preparation?

> Write out a brief schedule showing when you can allocate that amount of time for study.

> Ask God to help you follow through on using this time for study.

2. A professor once said, "When God tells your students to wiggle, don't you dare tell them to sit still." We need to select methods that are appropriate to the age level we teach. Methods that lead our students into discovery of God's truth are preferable to methods that always place the

39

teacher in the role of information-giver with students as passive receivers.

What is the method you most commonly use?

Is this a "delivery of content" method or a "leading in discovery" method?

What other methods could you use to promote greater interaction among students and help lead them into discovering God's truth from His Word?

Sometimes, in spite of excellent preparation and appropriate methods, students still are rude and unruly. If you have such students in your class, you must find a way to control them or you will endanger the learning experience of everyone in the class. Teachers always should be firm and consistent, but kind, in approaching students.

Ask God to give you a genuine love for your students, even the problem pupils. And along with doing all in your power, some teachers have found that enlisting specific prayer partners produces amazing results.

3. Make a list of those students who are rude, unruly, or frequently disrupt the class.

Find at least two other Christians who will covenant to pray for you and each student during the time that you prepare to teach and also when you actually are teaching. After class is over, be sure to give a report to your prayer partners and instruct them what to pray for specifically for the coming lesson. List your prayer partners.

In order to recognize how God helps you in your teaching, keep a journal of how your problem students respond each week in class.

Problem Student   Prayer Request   Response

Also record in your journal the amount of time you actually spend in preparation and the methods you use each week. By reviewing these journal entries, you will begin to notice patterns that can guide you in future preparation and teaching.

41

3

Teaching through Relationships

Several years ago I served as Minister of Education in a local church. Since we had no youth director, I filled that role also.

Shortly after I began working with the teens, it seemed obvious that if I wanted to get to know the high school students well, I needed an effective strategy. And so I decided to meet with each student individually for breakfast. We could talk together informally and build a closer relationship. And I could better understand the needs and interests of each person. After picking up the teen at home, we went out to a restaurant for breakfast, spent some time chatting, and then I dropped the student at school.

I confess that I was somewhat surprised by the reaction of the first student I invited to breakfast.

Steve didn't say anything, but pierced me with a rather quizzical stare. At last he replied, "Well, I guess that would be okay."

Somewhat less than unbridled enthusiasm, to say the least. And when we met at five 'til seven on Monday morning, he was not any more talkative. Which was understandable since 7:00

a.m. is still the night before to most teens.

We rode to the restaurant in silence. When we arrived, the manager was just getting ready to open the door, and so we waited for a moment.

Finally, Steve broke the silence. "Why are you doing this?" he demanded. "Have you been talking to my old man?"

"If you mean your father," I replied, "no. Why? Is there something I should know?"

"No, that's okay," he muttered.

As we were being seated (the first guests in the restaurant, I might add), Steve again demanded, "What are you doing this for? Are you sure you haven't been talking to my old man?"

"I'm meeting with you just because I want to get to know you better. And, no, your dad and I haven't talked—but I think we should."

After taking our seats, we scanned the menu and placed our orders. Again Steve broke the silence. "Who's paying for this?" he demanded.

"I am."

"You must have been talking to my old man."

"No, we haven't talked—yet, but you can be sure we will."

As I reminisce about our dialogue, I continue to be amazed at Steve's incredulity. He found it difficult to believe that I wanted to spend time with him, just getting to know him. And the fact that I even was willing to pay the bill for breakfast was the most incredible part of all.

But the brief time spent with my students in just such informal settings, and the few dollars invested, produced great dividends in my ministry with those teens.

When I try to impress upon teachers the important role that quality interaction plays in effective instruction, many assume that my suggestions are too simplistic—it has to be more complex than that. And so they look for deeper, more profound suggestions. While many of these ideas are not wrong, in and of themselves, they do complicate a fairly simple process.

Consider some of the suggestions that masquerade as the "key to effective teaching."

ERROR NUMBER ONE. "Quality teaching depends on how much the teacher knows."

If, indeed, this is the "key," then an obvious conclusion would be that the teacher who knows the most will be the best teacher automatically.

The error here is painfully obvious to all frustrated students who have sat under learned instructors who could not communicate their wealth of knowledge. On the other hand, ignorance is not an asset in teaching either. Quality teachers must know what they are trying to teach, and procrastinating until the last minute to begin preparing contributes little to a teacher's knowledge. Teachers must know the subject they teach, but quality teaching requires more than knowledge.

ERROR NUMBER TWO. "Quality teaching requires long periods of time spent in preparation."

At first glance, this seems plausible, because

most teachers spend too little time preparing their lessons. And, it is true that when too little time has been allocated to preparation, more time, appropriately spent, will improve instruction. However, this is valid only to a point.

Extreme time spent preparing usually leads a teacher to try to include more content. And rarely do students learn more when a teacher covers a great amount of material. The amount of information that we can teach depends every bit as much on the students as on the teacher. Jesus, the Master Teacher, told his followers, "I have yet many things to say unto you, but ye cannot bear them now" (John 16:12). On another occasion Jesus taught them clearly and yet Luke stated in three different ways that the disciples were not able to understand His teaching (Luke 18:34).

ERROR NUMBER THREE. "Quality teaching is determined by the number and the quality of creative methods used in the teaching/learning process."

This is not to demean the importance of high quality, creative methods, but some teachers develop an entertainment mentality. And the "creative methods" approach to effective teaching may imply that what the teacher does is the most important element in quality instruction. Actually, what the student does is far more important than what the teacher does. The teacher's methods take on meaning and value as they help students learn and apply the principles of godly living.

Quality teaching demands more than extensive

knowledge by the teacher, extensive time spent in preparation, or creative and varied teaching methods. High quality teaching occurs when a teacher cultivates quality relationships with students so that by using appropriate teaching methods, that teacher can help individual students know and do what God wants.

Notice that this definition includes four key elements. It includes quality relationships, appropriate methods, and then knowledge followed by behavior. Each of these elements is important. And as we consider cultivating relationships, we will see how getting to know our students contributes to the other three elements in this definition.

As I suggested in the beginning of this chapter, building relationships contributes significantly to effective teaching. What happens outside the classroom often determines the quality of what transpires in the classroom. When the Apostle Mark described the beginning of Jesus' ministry, he explained that Jesus called the disciples first to be "with Him" (Mark 3:14). And as Jesus built personal relationships with His followers, He was able to share with them the knowledge that they needed and then guide them into godly behavior.

BUILDING RELATIONSHIPS OUTSIDE OF CLASS

PLAN CLASS ACTIVITIES. There are countless activities that we can plan with our students.

Picnics, hikes, field trips, parties, games, sightseeing, and many other informal group meetings can provide times of fun and relationship-building. Social events can be as extensive as a camping trip or as simple as getting together for frozen yogurt. And one great feature of such group activities is that all but the youngest children can assist in planning and carrying them out. Not only does getting the student involved in planning ensure a higher level of involvement, it also lessens the burden for the teacher.

ATTEND THEIR ACTIVITIES. Most recently I have taught sixth-grade boys in Sunday School. Since most of them were soccer players, I was able to get to know them better and cultivate quality relationships by attending their soccer matches. You can't imagine how appreciative my students' parents were when they noticed me at their sons' activities. Attending school plays, musical events, various competitions, and other activities is valuable also in teaching children and youth. Visiting your adult students at work or attending church or community programs where they are involved likewise helps to build relationships.

SPEND TIME WITH STUDENTS INDI-VIDUALLY. I was able to get to know Steve, and many other teens, by occasionally sharing breakfast with them. Other teachers have met their students after school for a soft drink and some conversation. Since most adults eat lunch anyway, a lunch meeting can provide good interaction time, too. A round of golf, several sets of tennis, jogging, walking, or just "sitting in a rocking chair" can lay the foundation for quality ministry. With just a little imagination, you probably can create a list of potential activities several pages long for whatever age group you teach.

PLAN GROUP MINISTRY/SERVICE PROJECTS. Recently, I listened to a young adult reminiscing about a particularly effective teacher. This person shared the profound influence of the worship services that her class conducted once a month at the local nursing home. Not only did the class build relationships by planning and leading the service together, but they were able, also, to share the love of Christ with deeply appreciative, lonely invalids.

Service projects provide vital functions needed in the church, and they also can help church members or others who have specific, unmet needs. Older children, for example, can help to clean or decorate their classroom; teens can provide lawn care for senior adults. The men in one adult class that I know of offer tuneups and minor car repairs on Saturdays for single adults or elderly church members who need help.

But we are not limited to building relationships outside of class.

Our selection of teaching methods, attitude toward the students, and our whole approach to teaching helps us cultivate effective teacher/student relationships.

48

BUILDING RELATIONSHIPS DURING CLASS TIME

LISTEN TO STUDENTS. This means more than just giving polite attention to what your students say. An excellent way to get interaction and build relationships is to ask questions. But many teachers err in how they handle answers.

At one extreme is the teacher who can barely let the student finish an answer before paraphrasing and elaborating on that answer. This is nothing more than manipulation. The other extreme is saying nothing and ignoring the comment. Between these extremes is a balance of active listening where you express appreciation for the answer and encourage other students to interact.

But what about answers that are "off the wall"— answers that seem to miss the point of the question totally? I have found that these are rare. Often the answer only seems wrong. One wise approach is to ask the person to explain or elaborate on their reply. Usually, either the question was misunderstood or the student giving the answer has insight and understanding extending far beyond what the teacher expected. And if the answer really is totally wrong, encouraging others to add to the answer or to clarify will reinforce that you do value the person and the contribution. This promotes healthy relationships, encouraging future interaction.

DON'T GIVE ALL THE ANSWERS. It may seem appropriate for the teacher always to give the answer when students ask questions in class. But often it's wiser to resist that temptation. Rather, try to redirect those questions back to the class. This takes you, the teacher, out of the position of being the only authority, and it encourages students to recognize that they can find answers themselves. Obviously, a teacher should clarify misunderstanding or wrong answers, but this should be done with tact and appreciation for individual students and their answers.

ENCOURAGE SMALL TALK. Don't ever assume that every statement you make should sound as though it were etched in stone. Listen to your students and talk with them. As they arrive, chat about what has been happening in their worlds. And share what's been going on in yours. Treat them as real people who have real interests and concerns. Often you will find that the small talk will lead naturally into the lesson. And I can think of no better lesson introduction than natural, normal conversation leading into meaningful learning activities.

ENJOY TEACHING YOUR CLASS. Approach class in a relaxed manner. Ask God to free you from feeling tense or uptight. As humor arises in class, enjoy it. Obviously humor can get out of hand, but it is more common to find that a church classroom is a dreary, humorless place. When you make mistakes (and we all do, I guarantee), enjoy them with the class. All of us need to learn to laugh at ourselves. And our students usually delight in helping to teach us that lesson. If we are willing to recognize our own errors, we teach valuable lessons in transparency and vulnerability.

Christian education is serious business. I can think of nothing more important to which we could dedicate our lives. And that should never imply drudgery or tedium. Since one of the things that can contribute most to the teaching/learning process is building meaningful relationships with our students, we need to know them as individuals—as real people. And they should get to know us in the same way. When such relationships exist, the chance of meaningful learning in class increases dramatically. When that happens, the Holy Spirit can work through us most effectively to influence those students for Christ.

CONSIDER GOD'S WORD

Paul did more than just tell his students what God wanted them to do. He shared his life with them, but others also played a vital role in ministering to them.

Read through **II Timothy 1:2-7**. List the people mentioned in these verses who contributed to Timothy's development.

II Timothy 1:2. How did Paul describe Timothy?

How do you think he and Timothy developed such a relationship? What would characterize it?

How would Paul's relationship with Timothy help him to understand better who God is and how God relates to us?

II Timothy 1:3-4. What statements in these verses give us a clue to the kind of relationship Paul had with Timothy?

What did Paul do for Timothy even when they were apart from each other?

II Timothy 1:5-6. Timothy's parents both are mentioned in Acts 16:1. His mother had become a Christian, perhaps under Paul's instruction. We know very little about Timothy's father. He was a Greek, and we assume that he was not a believer. How does the mention of Timothy's mother and grandmother in II Timothy 1:5, help to emphasize the importance of godly influence?

Why do you think Paul urged Timothy to "stir up the gift of God" in him?

Apparently, Paul had helped to ordain Timothy to ministry. How could this have contributed to the special relationship they shared?

II Timothy 1:7. What did Paul say was not characteristic of a growing, godly person?

What three characteristics are appropriate?

How would the relationships mentioned in the previous verses contribute to these positive qualities in a Christian's life?

CONSIDER YOUR MINISTRY

1. List some people who have established close spiritual relationships with you.

How and what have they contributed to your

life and spiritual development?

What do you think they gained from the relationship?

2. Whom do you know well enough to encourage in their spiritual lives?

How did you get to know them?

How are you presently ministering to them?

3. Think of the students you teach. List those with whom you have made a good start in relationship-building.

Which students need more attention from you?

List some specific activities or general strategies that you can follow that will help you relate to them.

Pray and ask God to work in and through your life as you seek to minister through quality relationships with your students. Also thank Him for those who have contributed to your development. (And it wouldn't hurt to thank them, too.)

4

How to Grow a Student

I enjoy living things. I like to feed whatever birds we can attract to our back yard. I enjoy watching and encouraging the growth of the trees, shrubs, and flowers that surround our house. Often when I'm out backpacking or canoeing, I travel pretty slowly because I stop to examine the flora and fauna. Sitting in a canoe watching beavers at work or perched on a rock observing marmots are pleasant ways to spend an afternoon.

And I really don't like to leave growing things behind when I go indoors. At one time in my office there were plants on the floor, plants hanging from the ceiling, and plants on the cabinets in front of the windows.

One of the plants, a schefflera, grew for well over fifteen years. But it survived for that long only because I discovered the kind of attention that it needed—intentional neglect. When I watered it regularly, it was well on the way to an early demise. I had to discipline myself to water it no more than once every two weeks. Any more often and it lost leaves faster than they could be replaced. The soil needed to dry out as much as possible without dehydrating the plant.

At the other extreme was my hybrid croton. As soon as the soil began to dry out the croton sheds its leaves. But with a regular, ample water supply it thrived beautifully.

One plant needed minimal water in order to survive. The other demanded a large, regular supply. If I had switched procedures, both would have died quickly. The wrong kind of attention proves just as lethal as outright neglect. In order to nurture plants to growth, our care must be appropriate to the demands of that particular variety.

Our students also need to be nurtured. And what is appropriate nurture for one student could be counterproductive for another. This means that we need to know our students well enough to understand what will promote learning for each one.

When it comes to teaching, perhaps the key word is *motivation.*

Students who are motivated will learn. And learning is a satisfying, self-perpetuating activity. A person who feels that he or she is learning will be motivated to learn more. Then, that person will work harder at learning. And a person who works hard at learning will learn even more. A student in this cycle (motivation > hard work > achievement > increased motivation) will continue to learn because these drives come from within. This kind of self-sustaining motivation is called *Intrinsic Motivation.*

There is another kind of motivation, unfortunately, much more commonly used by educators—*Extrinsic Motivation.* Let's look at both types of motivation and the ways each might be seen in a Sunday School classroom.

EXTRINSIC MOTIVATION

Extrinsic motivation can take two forms—either negative or positive.

Basically, negative external motivation is punishment. We can tell a child that if he doesn't take out the trash, we will punish him. And in some cases it works—to a small degree, for a short period of time. But what happens when the threat of punishment is removed? The child often forgets the chore.

Of course Sunday School teachers can't threaten to punish students overtly. We tend do it less obviously—by withholding approval, by intimidation, or even by humiliation. Often a student who reports that, "My teacher doesn't like me" has experienced negative extrinsic motivation. Not only is this unkind, but usually it is counterproductive. Negative *extrinsic* motivation actually destroys *intrinsic* motivation.

But what about *positive* extrinsic motivation—some sort of a reward or prize for learning?

One of our sons came home from junior high school and informed us that his friend's father agreed to pay $50 for every "A" on his son's report card in an attempt to motivate the son to study. Our family all agreed that this was a safe offer, since even one "A" was unlikely for this student. And the promise of a reward was no more motivating to this student than the threats of punishment had been earlier.

Extrinsic motivation can take various forms in Sunday School, too. Some teachers might give candy bars to the well-behaved students. Or they may give $5 to each student bringing a Bible every Sunday throughout the year.

One Sunday School planned a recruitment contest: each student who brought a visitor received one dollar, and the student who brought the most visitors also received a camera. At the end of the contest, the visitors were counted and a young girl who had earned $20 won the camera. When asked how she was able to bring so many visitors, she explained that it was easy. She paid each of her friends 50 cents to come to Sunday School, pocketing the other 50 cents; and she won the camera, too. When asked about her relationship with Christ, she responded that she wasn't a Christian and didn't want to become one. But she *was* a shrewd business person.

The problem with positive extrinsic motivation is that it tends to be temporary. As long as a chance for a prize or reward exists, a person may work at learning. And some learning actually may occur. But when the external promise is removed, learning generally ceases.

Extrinsic motivation, whether negative or positive, is of minimal value to an excellent teacher. The excellent teacher seeks to trigger internal motivation. That inner, self-sustaining drive helps a person to become an independent learner who continues to learn long after the class is over and the teacher has gone.

INTRINSIC MOTIVATION

Intrinsic motivation could be likened to inertia in the physical world. When we study the laws of motion in physics class, we learn that an object at rest remains at rest unless acted upon by some external force. That is why a car sitting in a level driveway with the engine turned off will not go anywhere unless some force causes it to do so. The other half of this law explains that an object in motion will remain in motion unless acted upon by some external force. This means that once an automobile is moving, it will keep going forever unless some force acts upon it to slow it down and stop it—which, in fact, happens. The external force is friction: friction in the wheel bearings, friction on the highway, even the friction of air around the car. It is inertia that causes the foolish passenger who refuses to wear a seat belt to continue to move forward into the windshield if the car stops suddenly in an accident.

Our students are either at rest or in motion, too. We refer to one who is at rest as unmotivated. Conversely, a motivated student is one in motion— a student who has come to love learning, seeking answers, exploring the world of ideas, asking questions, and challenging what a teacher may say. A motivated student is a delight to teach.

Unfortunately, most students don't come to us internally motivated. So it is up to us to discover ways to trigger that intrinsic, internal motivation.

The following suggestions for stimulating internal motivation have helped many teachers. Perhaps they will strengthen your ministry, too.

Set Worthwhile Goals. An excellent way to trigger a student's internal motivation is to help that student see that there is a reason to learn something. If students see no reason to learn, they will have little or no motivation to do so. A common complaint by students in math or history courses is that they will never use what they have learned. Therefore, they reason, why bother learning it in the first place?

Do we ever teach the Bible only as history? If we fail to demonstrate the relevance of what we are teaching, students may view Scripture as nothing more than ancient facts. And, consequently, they may have a low level of motivation, not having a reason to learn, having no worthwhile goal. So our task is to show how the Scripture and scriptural principles explained by Bible facts apply to real life. A teacher who fails to apply Scripture lessons to life has done only a partial job.

Address Felt Needs. Teaching to felt needs has much in common with giving students worthwhile goals. Students who know that they have a problem often come to your class looking for a solution. Such students are highly motivated learners.

Suppose that you are teaching a course in first aid. On the way to class, your students pass the scene of a horrible automobile accident where people are injured and need help. When your students arrive, you can be sure that they will be extremely motivated—have a high felt need—to learn about first aid.

But most Sunday School students don't have such strongly felt spiritual needs. Their internal motivation is relatively low. An effective way to teach such students is to take time in the lesson introduction to help them recognize their needs. Then, in the course of teaching the lesson, you may demonstrate how God's Word speaks to those needs. When students grasp the fact that the Bible really does relate to life—their lives—they may become highly motivated, independent learners.

Stimulate Curiosity. Most people are naturally curious. If the phone rings and someone else in the family answers, we usually want to know who called. When flying in an airplane, we find it difficult not to glance over and see what the person sitting next to us is reading. And an open diary laying on a table is a challenge that few can resist.

But many teachers fail to take advantage of this inner drive. We treat the most exciting message in the world—God's revealed truth—in a ho-hum, prosaic manner. We need to share the adventure of the Word. We need to raise questions in the minds of our students—questions that will draw us into God's Word for answers. In the introduction to a lesson, we can pose a problem or present a paradox. Then, in the course of the lesson, we can help students discover the answers to those questions that we raised at the beginning of class.

Provide Adequate Challenge. Many people rise to a challenge, especially those who are comfortable with themselves or who feel competent to face the unknown or unexpected. Many years ago we learned that Mark, our oldest son, had this tendency. He has accomplished certain things that he later admitted having attempted simply because we had told him they were very hard to do. Just to prove that he could succeed, Mark worked extra hard at the challenge.

Wise teachers get to know their students well enough so that they can tell how each will respond to a challenge. The same challenge that triggers motivation in one student may overwhelm another, so challenge must be geared to the level and ability of each individual.

For example, a student with good literary skills and a knowledge of how to use resource books may well be motivated to discover how many mountains are mentioned in the Bible. Adults often respond to a challenge to research a particular topic and share their discovery with class members. When I was a junior in a Vacation Bible School, I learned more than a hundred verses in one week just because I wanted to out-memorize a friend. There was a challenge and I responded to it.

We must be careful not to challenge students beyond their ability and cause frustration. But, on the other hand, we must never manipulate or take unfair advantage of students who are highly motivated by a challenge.

Cultivate Personal Relationships. Each of the

64

preceding techniques is a valuable tool for stirring intrinsic motivation. But perhaps the greatest motivator of all is a relationship of love and respect between teacher and student. More than one student has become excited about God's Word because a teacher loved that student. When love and concern are communicated, students become excited about what excites the teacher.

As we considered in an earlier chapter, teachers develop personal relationships by spending time with our students, taking an interest in who they are and what they are doing. Expressing sincere appreciation and compliments also builds respect and relationships. And as relationships grow, learning increases, too. Our students are highly motivated when we trigger their intrinsic motivation.

Do you have some students who are objects in motion? Rejoice in that fact and aim them in the right direction. With a little encouragement, they may well amaze you and others with their excitement and willingness to learn. Your biggest problem will be coming up with appropriate projects for them to do. They will challenge you.

But most of your students probably will be objects at rest. Indeed, some may seem more like stone statues than living beings. But they don't have to remain that way. Your objective is to find the right trigger for each student, even though it may be deeply hidden by years of indifferent teaching that has stifled their inner motivation.

The motivation trigger will be different for each

student, but it is there. Once you discover it, take advantage of the marvelous drives that God has built into all children, youth, and adults. Stimulate a student's intrinsic motivation and you will be well along the way to growing an individual who will blossom and bear fruit to the glory of God for years to come.

CONSIDER GOD'S WORD

Jesus Christ was an outstanding Teacher who triggered intrinsic motivation. Jesus constantly challenged His followers to think through difficult concepts. He gave them assignments that stretched their creativity. In some cases, the only solution was to come back to Him for help in accomplishing the task assigned to them. Whether asking His disciples to feed 5,000 or to cross a lake in a violent storm, Jesus stirred the internal motivation of His followers. He regularly reminded them of how important it was to rely upon Him to help solve their problems.

The Apostle Paul also taught effectively. Let's consider some of the devices that Paul employed as triggers for internal motivation.

Read *I Thessalonians 2:1-13.* Notice how often Paul dealt with the concept of motivation in these verses. First, Paul explained his own motivation— why he acted the way he did. Then he also explained how he triggered internal motivation on the part of the Thessalonian believers.

I Thessalonians 2:3-6. List actions or attitudes that demonstrate what motivated Paul in his relationship with the Thessalonians.

    2:3 —

    2:4 —

    2:5 —

    2:6 —

ILLUSTRATION ONE. The way in which a mother relates to her newborn infant is one way Paul chose to illustrate how he related to the Thessalonians. This illustration is found in chapter 2, verses 7-9.

I Thessalonians 2:7-8. In what ways could Paul be likened to a mother?

How does this gentle, sensitive description seem to contradict other impressions we might have of Paul?

I Thessalonians 2:9-10. Apparently Paul did not receive offerings from the Thessalonians while he remained there teaching them (verse 9). Rather, he worked hard to support himself financially so that he could stay and teach God's Word. How do you think Paul felt about supporting himself?

Why do you think he brought up the subject?

How did Paul's behavior demonstrate a selfless, giving spirit?

In what ways would Paul's selfless "mother-like" attitude have triggered spiritual motivation among the Thessalonians?

ILLUSTRATION TWO. The second illustration Paul used is a description of how a father relates to his children. Three key words describe this relationship. "Exhort" means to encourage a person to act or behave in a certain way. "Comfort" means to encourage, especially with consideration given to emotions, how a person feels about doing something. And "charge" means to call one to live in a purposeful, goal-oriented manner. How do these three words seem appropriate for you as a teacher or leader?

Exhort —

Comfort —

Charge —

I Thessalonians 2:12-13. What was the purpose Paul had in mind for relating to his students as he did?

And what was the outcome in their lives?

CONSIDER YOUR MINISTRY

As we minister to our students, we need to consider the topic of motivation. Our own motivation should be the first consideration. Then, we also need to consider how we will choose to trigger our students' motivation.

1. Why do you serve in the ministry that you do?

> In what ways do your actions demonstrate your motivation for ministry?

> List any changes you might make in your behavior in order to show your motivation more appropriately.

2. In what way could the illustration of a mother be appropriate to describe how you relate to your students?

List anything that might hinder building quality relationships with the individuals you teach.

What steps can you take to improve these areas?

3. Are you challenging your students as a father challenges his children? Give examples of how you have challenged your students.

What responses have you seen in your students' lives? (Compare the Thessalonians in verse 13.)

What can you do to challenge further the students in your ministry?

5

Teaching the Great Stone Face

Some time ago I asked a teacher how his class was going.

"I wish I knew," he replied. "But no one says anything. My students just sit there and stare at me. I feel as though I'm trying to teach 'The Great Stone Face'."

Unfortunately, he is not alone. Other teachers also face tuned-out, uninvolved students. No one seems to be quite sure how and when this attitude begins, but it does.

Some teachers think that people are born that way, but we have much evidence to the contrary. Others blame it on Sunday School teachers, but it's a problem in other settings, too. There are teachers who think that it happens only when *they* teach. But that suggests these teachers haven't observed other classes and what happens in them. Some educators suggest that we teachers, and our teaching methods, may be a contributing factor. And perhaps others would go even further, calling us the chief culprits.

Whether it's in the Sunday School or the public school classroom, somehow students get the idea that learning is a passive activity. At some point in the process of formal education, a person may stop participating in class and just sit there.

And we wonder what causes it.

But why not find out for yourself when passivity attacks?

Take a tour through your Sunday School and find out what is going on. You may gain interesting insights to help you understand the problem and, perhaps, a solution.

Look at a Preschool class. What are they doing? They may be enthusiastically singing "Jesus Loves Me." Or doing finger plays. Or "listening" to a Bible story by giving the teacher frequent and insistent suggestions on how to tell it. Perhaps they have put their chairs in a row and are "riding a bus" to Sunday School. Whatever they are doing, you can be sure that it is active. They are involved and enthusiastic. And there is an exuberance that may leave you breathless.

Drop in on the Primaries. They, too, will be active. Some may be asking questions. Others, bursting with excitement, will wave their hands frantically to be called on. They may be practicing a skit, or they may be working out of their student manuals. But they won't be passive, and they rarely are quiet.

The Juniors are delightful. They are full of questions—bright and cheerful. They want to know why things are the way they are and what they should do about it. The teacher probably won't ask them rhetorical questions, since they tend to answer whether you want them to or not.

They will be active, excited, and alive.

But look at the Junior Highers, a very different story. They often sit staring glumly at the teacher—or at nothing. Often the teacher's questions are answered only by the teacher. And so the teacher may have resorted to lecture, grinding it out week after week.

Many times the High School class is no better, following the pattern of the younger teen class.

It is unfortunate, but most adult teachers also approach class, armed with their teacher's manuals, presuming that they are the sole source of knowledge. Such teachers seem to view their primary responsibility as dispensing information—one application a week, with the dosage dictated by the length of class time remaining after the "preliminaries" are over.

Once the coffee and donuts are put away, praise and prayer notes shared, upcoming birthdays and anniversaries remembered, missionaries prayed for, attendance and offering taken, the next social planned, and miscellaneous announcements made, the teacher is allotted a token amount of time to "give the lesson." And give it he or she does.

Since there may be so little time, and since there is so much information to give, all the teacher can imagine doing is lecturing at top speed. "The lesson" stands out in marked contrast to the rest of the class session. Usually there is interaction and participation during the "preliminaries." But when the teacher stands up, usually all involvement comes to a screeching stop.

What has happened? Think back to the

Preschool and early elementary classes. What did we observe? There was student interaction, wasn't there? The learners were involved, active, participating. But we seem to forget that important element in the teaching/learning process when we get to the teen years and beyond. Many teachers assume that youth and adults learn passively, with learners serving as receivers and the teacher as a transmitter.

There is another interesting phenomenon that takes place in the younger age classes.

You may have noticed that some teachers in these departments were trying to discourage student involvement. Some of the teachers may have been trying to "maintain order"—repeatedly reminding their students to sit down and be quiet.

Now, this doesn't work with Preschoolers. And Primaries and Juniors usually don't keep quiet much better. But after years of being told to keep quiet in class, by the time learners reach the teen years, the message seems to have sunk in.

So it is no wonder that teen and adult learners are often passive. They may prefer to sit back and see what the teacher has to offer—what kind of a lesson has been prepared, and how it will be delivered.

Really good teachers usually do not allow themselves to be manipulated into simply dispensing information to passive receivers. They know that the key to effective learning is involvement, so they work to get students involved. And they recognize that there are at least three ways to secure that involvement.

INVOLVE STUDENTS BY ADDRESSING
FELT NEEDS

First, we can teach in such a way that we meet the felt needs of our students. This means that our instruction speaks to those issues where students know that they have problems and are looking for answers.

Let's look at an example of teaching to felt needs. Again, assume that you are teaching a class on first aid techniques. Today's lesson deals with CPR (cardio-pulmonary resuscitation). Just as your class members are entering the building, one of them has a heart attack. With a sense of desperation, fellow class members frantically await the arrival of the emergency squad. When the paramedics arrive, they do all they can to save his life. But it is too late. In sorrow and frustration the paramedics turn to the crowd. "Why didn't anyone here administer CPR?" they ask. "If any of you here knew CPR, and had helped this person, he probably would be alive right now."

Picture class members as they enter the room and relate to you all that has happened. You would not need to figure out how to get them interested in learning CPR technique. They would come, motivated by a felt need. And all that you would have to do is respond to that need. There is no question that the class would be highly motivated to learn.

Unfortunately, such a level of desire to learn spiritual truths is relatively uncommon. Therefore, we cannot rely on students coming to class already interested in the lesson that we have prepared.

INVOLVE STUDENTS BY USING ALL FIVE SENSES

Many research projects have addressed the question of how students learn. One particular project analyzed college students who wanted to learn (those two don't always go together). These students were taught through a variety of techniques. Teachers taught using words alone. Then they taught using visual methods. Finally, visual and verbal methods were combined.

When teachers used words alone, they found that students tested three days later had retained only about ten percent of the material. When teachers used visual methods, three-day retention doubled to twenty percent. But when verbal and visual were combined, retention was five times as great as with words alone—about fifty percent.

This bears out a basic principle of communication. The more of our senses that are employed, the greater impact the instruction has.

Suppose I were watering my garden with a single hose, complaining to you that it was terribly inefficient. If you looked at the back of my house and saw four more faucets with hoses coiled next to them, you would want to know why I didn't use the other four hoses. "Oh, it's too much work to hook them up, and uncoil the hoses," I would reply. And you would walk off shaking your head!

But teachers do it all the time. We could get our

79

students involved by employing all five senses. But we often resort to the old standby and turn on the lecture faucet, even though the hose attached to it may be worn and leaky.

INVOLVE STUDENTS THROUGH DYNAMIC INTERACTION

It is important to try always to address our students' felt needs. And we should use a variety of methods to involve as many senses as possible. But we can go beyond that. We can get our students interacting with each other and with us, the teacher.

Dynamic methods are those that take advantage of group interaction. These are methods such as question/answer, discussion, brainstorming, and buzz groups.

If we examine the teaching methods of Christ, it soon becomes obvious that He did more than lecture. He told stories and used object lessons. "Behold the fowls of the air....Consider the lilies of the field..." (Matthew 6:26,28). And Christ used dynamic interaction, too. He asked His disciples questions, and He taught in a way that prompted them to ask Him questions. He discussed ideas with them and explained difficult concepts that they did not understand.

We would do well to model our teaching after Christ. Some of the most effective learning takes place as students interact with other learners. As we employ methods that encourage regular interaction among our students and with us as teachers, students become involved. And involvement is a key to effective learning.

As students grow older, they do not need to become passive learners. We can plan teaching methods to involve all ages, from the youngest to the oldest. But it does take some effort and some planning. We need to know our students well enough to be able to address their felt needs through our instruction. We need to look for creative ways to employ senses other than the sense of hearing. But let's not stop with that. We also can use dynamic methods that encourage meaningful interaction with each other and with us.

And then we won't find ourselves teaching to "The Great Stone Face."

CONSIDER GOD'S WORD

Most of us never think about the teaching style of Jesus. Although many theses and dissertations have been written about His methodology, very little of it has been published for the average reader. In order to learn about Jesus' style, we need to read through the Gospels thinking more about His methods than about the content of His instruction. Usually, we focus only on the content, but as you read through the following passages, don't just think about the messages that Jesus communicated. Instead, also notice how He taught. Consider the method as well as the message.

Read **Matthew 13:1-52.** Make a list of the stories (parables) that Jesus used in these verses.

As children, many of us learned that a parable is "an earthly story with a heavenly meaning." It is a good story that stands alone, but there also are spiritual truths that the story teaches. The earthly meaning of the story usually is straightforward, but the spiritual meaning may be hidden to those who are spiritually blind.

Matthew 13:10. What does verse 10 indicate about the disciples' understanding of Jesus' teaching methods?

Matthew 13:11. What special relationship did the disciples have to Jesus and to His teaching?

Matthew 13:11-12. In what ways did following Jesus demonstrate that the disciples had some level of spiritual insight?

Matthew 13:16-18. What additional insight did they receive (see, too, the parallel passage in Mark 4:10-12) because of their relationship with Jesus?

Matthew 13:13-15. But everyone did not respond the way the disciples did. Those who were spiritually blind failed to see the spiritual truths that the parables contained. Because the unbelievers already had rejected Jesus' teaching, the more they heard, the more they hardened their hearts. Do people today show similar response to the truth? How?

Matthew 13:18-23. How does the interpretation of the Parable of the Sower relate to the teaching about the hard hearts (verse 15) of those who rejected Jesus' teaching?

Into which category do you think the disciples fit?

Which kind of soil described the Pharisees?

To which category do you think the majority of the multitude (Matthew 13:2) belonged?

Another of Jesus' approaches to teaching was to give His disciples a project to do. Sometimes they were able to carry out the assignment; other times they had to come back to Jesus for help and further instruction.

Read *Mark 6:33-44.* How did Jesus' solution to the people's hunger (verse 37) differ from the disciples' (verse 36).

What resources did Jesus possess to feed the multitude? (John 6:9 explains the source of the small amount of food that they did have.)

What did He do with it?

Why do you think that Jesus told His disciples to feed the multitude even though

85

He knew that they would not be able to do it on their own?

What lesson do you think the disciples learned from this experience?

Most of the time Jesus did not give extended lectures to His followers. In fact, the Gospels only record three major sermons (the Sermon on the Mount, the Upper Room Discourse, and the Olivet Discourse). And these sermons include many illustrations, examples, and mini-parables. Scan through a portion of the Sermon on the Mount in Matthew 6:25-34. Remember that Jesus was standing on a hillside and many of the things that He talked about were all around them. List the illustrations from nature that He used.

Why do you think that Jesus used such illustrations?

How would these have added to the impact of His teaching?

How would such illustrations contribute to His followers' remembering His teaching in the future?

CONSIDER YOUR MINISTRY

The story is told about the pollster interviewing a homeowner in a major city.

"Which do you think is the greater problem in our country," asked the pollster, "ignorance or apathy?"

"I don't know, and I don't care" replied the interviewee.

I would suggest that both of these are problems in our classroom, too. The first problem, ignorance, is all too common. Students don't know the Word of God very well. And, unfortunately, sometimes the teacher is not much better prepared.

The second problem, apathy, often contributes to ignorance. If students are allowed to be passive learners, their apathy will reduce the chance of any true learning occurring. Excellent teachers know the value of getting students involved in the learning process. Think about how you and others have involved students in the lesson.

1. Need involvement means teaching to your students felt needs. When students see that instruction addresses *their* problems, they will respond and participate in the learning activities. And they will grow spiritually.

List some of the major needs of your students by individual name.

How does the Word of God speak to those needs?
Give specific examples for specific needs.

> How do you think your students would
> respond if they knew that they would receive
> biblical teaching that would address these
> needs each time they entered your class?

2. Sensory involvement means using techniques
that communicate to students through multiple
senses (taste, touch, sight, sound, smell).

Think back to a recent classroom experience. What
was the dominant method of instruction?

> How many senses did the students use in
> this class?

How could more senses have been used?

How would it have improved the lesson's effectiveness if multiple senses had been used in this class?

3. Dynamic involvement gets students involved though interaction with each other and with the teacher.

Why do you think there is so little discussion in many of our classes?

How do you think students would feel about class if they came knowing that they would be taught biblical concepts and then given the opportunity to interact with others about the meaning and application of those truths?

Which of the three types of involvement (need, sensory, dynamic) do you plan to use in the near future? How?

Pray and ask God to help you use these approaches effectively and to His glory.

6

Electronic Media for Christian Education

The story is told about the man who bought a mule from a shrewd farmer. Since he felt somewhat insecure, purchasing an animal known for its stubbornness, the man asked the farmer if the mule obeyed. He received full assurance that the mule was well-trained and responsive. Just to ease the purchaser's mind, the farmer even wrote out all of the commands that he had trained the mule to follow.

However, the first time that the man tried to work the mule, he was singularly unsuccessful. No matter what instruction he gave, and regardless of his tone of voice, the mule remained still as a statue. Finally, in total frustration, the buyer telephoned the farmer who agreed to see if he could help solve the problem.

When the farmer arrived, he tried all of the commands that the man had tried—with the same outcome. The mule ignored all attempts at persuasion. Finally, the farmer went to the lumber pile, picked up a two-by-four, walked back to the mule, and calmly dealt it a terrific blow across the forehead. He then gave a command which the mule followed immediately.

Needless to say, the mule's new owner was extremely upset.

"You told me that this mule was well trained and obedient," he said. "And now you hit him over the head to get him going. How can you say that he is obedient?"

"Oh, he *is* obedient," replied the farmer. "He does whatever you say. You just have to get his attention first."

Sooner or later, all of us who teach find ourselves in a situation like the mule's new owner. We know the principles of effective teaching. We have prepared well, and we know what we want to accomplish. But we may feel as though we need some strategy with the impact of a two-by-four to get our students' attention. Somehow we need to break through all of the clutter. We want to shout, "Wake up! Pay attention! These are the most important truths in the world."

Perhaps it's time to try a different approach. While there are obvious reasons why a literal two-by-four is inappropriate, *some* technique to get students' attention *does* make sense.

Most people who have spent any time at all in Sunday School expect Bible teachers to talk. And some of us do it with a vengeance! Then we're surprised when we can't compete with sports, school, work, television, popular music, friends, entertainment, and countless other topics vying for people's attention.

One way to grab our students' attention is to fight fire with fire. Since technology, especially the entertainment media, is such a powerful force today, it makes sense to use these same resources to promote effective Christian education. Occasionally, some teachers attempt visual methods such as flannelgraph, the chalkboard, or overhead projector. But the people we teach today live in a world characterized by *dramatic* technological innovation.

And the younger the child, the more that innovative technology is taken for granted. Most of us parents, at one time or another, have had to ask our children to help us program the VCR, explain how to use our computer software, or show us how to get the printer formatted properly.

Recently, while I was reading the manual for new computer software I had purchased, my son Mark informed me that he felt manuals were useless. He proclaimed that just sitting down and starting to use the program was far easier—and faster, too.

But there is one high-tech resource that any of us can use effectively for Christian education. And it's not even rocket science—no manual needed. The method that has tremendous potential for teaching today is *video*. I certainly am *not* suggesting replacing the teacher with a TV; instead, I recommend that we teachers use video to break through the clutter and communicate more effectively. Consider these suggested ways that we can take advantage of this resource for Christian education.

Video Instruction. Video is a powerful tool for

bringing outstanding teachers right into your classroom. But a word of caution: This does not mean using video *instead* of teaching. Those who have tried replacing a teacher with video have found that the novelty of sitting in class and watching a videotape only lasts for about three weeks.

Rather, what *is* effective is to use video teachers as a *resource* to assist the classroom teacher. The teacher still is needed to introduce the class, play the video, and lead in meaningful discussion and interaction with the video teacher's ideas. Playing a segment of a tape, and then pausing for group discussion and application, is often quite effective. Some teachers have used video for youth or adults in a large group presentation, followed by small group sessions for meaningful interaction.

Teacher Training. Many teachers, especially lay persons, have never been trained in effective teaching methods. Some have never even seen excellent teaching demonstrated. Video training resources can bring outstanding instruction right into your local church training classes. Instructors who might cost great sums of money to bring in can share their insights for only a few dollars on video. They will enliven your training sessions, and your teachers will benefit from their expertise.

Christian Drama. There is a growing wealth of high quality Christian entertainment. Much of it is more than entertaining; it is also instructional. By observing actors struggling with situations similar to those which all of us face, we can evaluate potential responses and their consequences. If the characters make the wrong choice, students can benefit by recognizing the decisions which led to the outcomes.

It is important not to watch the drama just as entertainment. While it is certainly that, it should be much more. Class discussion can help students learn far more than if they just watch the video and go home. Many teachers have found that Christian drama on video is a very desirable activity for socials, or even for having students into your home for a time of fun and relaxation.

Lesson Introductions. One of the primary tasks that every teacher faces is getting students' attention focused on desirable topics. When students arrive in class, their thoughts usually have little to do with that day's lesson. Carefully selecting a video segment of an appropriate illustration will help any teacher focus attention on the lesson.

Perhaps a scene from a Christian drama will function effectively. Or select something taped off the TV. Just be sure that the scene you select is appropriate to your class's maturity, effectively introduces the lesson, and is in good taste.

Group Discussion Situations. Effective group discussion demands that the teacher set the scene by presenting a situation that gives group members a reason to discuss it.

A scene presenting an ethical dilemma can easily

get adults discussing biblical principles. Teens who face difficult peer pressure will discuss a problem enthusiastically if a realistic dramatized conflict is used to present it. And children will recognize temptations to lie or steal when they observe other children struggling with the same issues. These and countless other scenes can be found in many Christian video presentations. Just ask your knowledgeable Christian bookstore or video supplier for suggestions of relevant tapes.

Dramatized Bible Stories. It is a struggle for any of us to understand the context and characteristics of events that took place thousands of years ago in another culture. For years we have used pictures and flannelgraph to teach Bible stories. Why not supplement these good tools with a video that shows the events as they happened?

Many teachers have found that segments from *Jesus of Nazareth* make Bible events come alive. If you have theological questions about the content of some video presentations, as I do, merely use the scenes that are relevant to your lesson. And you will have come a long way when you realize that, for instructional purposes, video cassettes rarely should be used from beginning to end without interruption. You are the teacher. You are in control. Use only the tape portion that you want—when you want to use it.

Children's Video. A wide variety of material appropriate for children currently is on the market. Animated Bible stories can be used to teach effectively. Dramatized or animated presentations of situations and circumstances that children encounter are valuable. For preschool children, animation is not even necessary. Testing with three to five year olds has demonstrated that video books and creative video taping of flat pictures is just as effective as animation. Often the simpler presentation is understood more easily by preschool children. Scenes that show what life was like in Bible times will communicate to children far more effectively than verbal descriptions ever can.

Missions Education. We encounter the same problems in missions education as we face in trying to explain what life was like when the Bible was written. A different life and culture are hard for both adults and children to understand. Drama, documentaries, and travelogues can be used effectively by the wise teacher for this crucial part of Christian education.

Dramatizations of missionary heroes bring them alive to people living today. Or, why not ask your church's missionaries to make video presentations of their life and ministry to share with class members? The video can be used by several, if not all, classes.

The video format from other countries may not be compatible with the U.S. format, but if the tape was made on equipment from this country, there will be no problem. You might suggest that your church provide a camcorder for your missionaries to use with their families. A valuable fringe benefit will be the timely information that can be shared with church members and Sunday School classes.

Desperate Circumstances. While I am reluctant to suggest this as a general rule, sometimes video can get you out of a jam. What if you find out on Sunday morning at five 'til classtime that a teacher is not going to show up? There is no substitute available, and you are hesitant or unable to combine classes. An appropriate videotape, selected from the church library, can be an excellent solution for a difficult problem.

You say that you have no church video library? For shame! Any Christian education leader of a church who hasn't begun a lending library of video cassettes should hang his head in disgrace. Video is here to stay. And wise church leaders recognize that fact. This is why so many churches now provide quality video resources for teachers, leaders, and families to use wherever appropriate. And this includes a last minute "fill-in" for an absentee teacher. It is better to have an adult monitor a video than to conscript a teacher unfamiliar with the lesson who cannot adequately teach God's holy Word.

Teaching is a calling. And effective teaching is imperative. But that doesn't mean each teacher has to be proficient in every communication skill that exists. The wise and effective teacher takes advantage of all kinds of resources available to promote quality instruction. We have a wonderful assortment of resources—and students who respond to each one. Don't overlook high-technology resources. Video cassettes are inexpensive and easy to use. What's more, they are unparalleled in some of the ways they can contribute to the teaching/learning process. Give video a try. You, and your students, will be glad that you did.

CONSIDER GOD'S WORD

Obviously there was no video or any other electronic media in the first century. But neither were there books, Sunday School curriculum, church buildings, pews or many other things that we regularly use in ministry today. However, the Bible does contain numerous examples of effective instructional methodology.

Perhaps none is more dramatic than the Jew's annual reenactment of the Passover dinner. When the Israelites were about to leave Egypt on their journey to the Promised Land, God instituted the Passover feast. This feast was highly symbolic and designed to remind and instruct God's people. It was a reminder in that it looked back to God's care for His people. God instructed parents to use the annual feast to remind their families of what He had done in delivering the Jews from the bondage of the Egyptians.

But the Passover also looked forward in symbolism. Various elements of the feast prepared the Israelites to understand what would happen when Jesus came to deliver God's people. Jesus came not to deliver from the enslavement of Egypt, but from the bondage of sin and death.

When parents and children observed the feast of Passover, they acted out a drama. This dramatic production taught each family member by reminding them of significant spiritual truths and providing the opportunity to discuss these concepts.

Read **Exodus 12:1-27.** If you have a commentary on the book of Exodus, read the appropriate portions. The *Ryrie Study Bible* also has valuable footnotes that will help to explain the profound significance of many elements of this feast.

Exodus 12:4. How would observing this feast promote family (and neighborly) togetherness?

Exodus 12:5-7. Perhaps the most significant of all the elements in the Passover observance was the selection and slaughter of the lamb. The lamb is a clear picture of Jesus Christ, the Lamb of God (John 1:29) who, hundreds of years later, was offered up as the sacrifice for our sins. Compare the New Testament passages with each of the Exodus verses that follow and list how the lamb was a picture of Jesus Christ.

Exodus 12:5 compared with I Peter 1:19.

Exodus 12:6 compared with John 12:23-24,27.

Exodus 12:7 compared with Hebrews 9:22.

Exodus 12:11. What was the symbolism in how the Israelites were to be dressed, and the attitude with which they were to eat the feast?

Exodus 12:14-17. How often and for how many years was the feast to be observed?

What was the purpose in the repeated observance?

Leaven (yeast) is a picture of sin in the Bible. What were the Jews to do with their leaven prior to the feast?

How can this symbol instruct us today?

Exodus 12:24-27. Why would the observance of the Passover be valuable for the Israelites once they had settled in the Promised Land?

Why was it so important that this be done regularly?

How would the annual observance set the stage for parents and children to discuss spiritual matters?

How would acting out the Passover serve as a more powerful teaching tool than merely having the parents lecture their children about what God had done for their ancestors?

There is a parallel to the Passover for us today. Read *Matthew 26:17-30*. Notice that Jesus observed the feast of Passover with His disciples just before He was taken to be crucified. At that

104

time He instituted what we have come to know as the Lord's Supper or communion. What parallels do you see between the two observances? (You may want to read I Corinthians 11:23-34.)

Matthew 26:26-28. What rememberance is there for us in the elements of the communion observance?

How can the Lord's Supper (communion) instruct us today even as the Passover taught the Israelites?

Why do we observe the Lord's Supper and not the Passover?

How would the drama and involvement of the events surrounding these observances make them meaningful learning experiences?

CONSIDER YOUR TEACHING

1. When adult teachers are questioned about instructional methods, they invariably rate lecture as one of the least effective methods, but the one that they use most often. Do you agree or disagree? Why would it be least effective?

Why do you think that most adults use lecture so often even though they recognize its significant limitations?

2. Think about how those whom you teach, or your fellow students, respond to various kinds of methodology. How do they respond when you use a straight lecture format?

What other methods do they prefer?

3. Think back to a recent lesson you taught or have observed being taught. What was the primary method used?

How did the students respond to the methodology?

List several ways that video could have been incorporated into the instructional methods used to teach that lesson.
    1.

2.

3.

How do you think the class would have responded if video methods had been used in class?

What do you plan to do about taking advantage of video methods for instructional purposes?

We Need Our
Sunday School!

Elaine and I are parents who are sold on Sunday School. We are committed to Sunday School because of what we have observed in our children's lives.

Unquestionably, we were personally accountable to God for our sons' Christian education. And yet we recognized that we needed help in teaching and guiding them. We could not possibly provide all of the spiritual instruction that our children needed, and Sunday School has been one of our key resources.

We enrolled each of our three boys soon after birth, and most of their church educational experiences have been positive. Even before our oldest son, Mark, knew how to talk, he became excited every time he rode in a car near our church. In fact, Mark enjoyed going to church so much it sometimes presented a problem. If we were out shopping and happened to drive past the church, Mark would become upset because we didn't stop and take him in to Sunday School. And we had similar experiences with Kevin and Nathan.

Our young sons were unaware of all that went

into Sunday School teaching, but they knew from their earliest years that church was a place where they were loved and accepted—a good place to go. We are delighted that our children could learn such a significant lesson very early in life.

Our sons are presently in their early 20s, in college or graduate school, but as they grew and matured, Sunday School relationships have contributed significantly to their spiritual development. Often as we discuss past teachers, our sons recall godly adults who have loved and supported them, many of whom express continuing interest in what they are doing now.

We are convinced that valuable Sunday School experiences don't happen automatically, though. They require attention and effort. And while teachers are very important, parents also play a crucial role in providing those experiences. Teachers need to be aware of how important parental cooperation is in Christian education.

Consider some of the strategies that helped to enrich our boys' Christian education experiences. Any of these that you can promote among parents of your students will dramatically increase your own teaching effectiveness.

LOOK AT SUNDAY SCHOOL THROUGH THE CHILDREN'S EYES

If we want to help children gain maximum value from Sunday School, we must view it through their eyes. This means giving them an opportunity to express what they feel. Parents and children must talk together about what goes on in Sunday School. But since many children may be like ours were, "How was Sunday School?" will be answered, "Fine." And the response to "What happened today?" will be, "Nothing."

Rather than starting with questions, often it is more productive for parents to talk about the good things that happened in their own classes. Then the children will be much more likely to comment on theirs. And, it is important not to criticize what children say. Instead, parents should listen and encourage them to share their experiences. Children need to feel free to express their views of Sunday School.

Parents should encourage each family member to participate in discussing experiences—any interesting or funny situations that came up in class, special illustrations, or new things that they may have learned. Parents probably will discover some elements in Sunday School that the children don't like. But that shouldn't surprise us, since no program is perfect. (And we all fall short of perfection as parents, too.) Just listening will encourage children to share their opinions openly. We must grant them that privilege.

As teachers, we need to encourage this kind of openness, too. How well do we work with the parents of our students? We are partners who need to understand each other and work together.

Recently, a friend of ours shared that his son was bored with Sunday School. This young teen had said that he was tired of drawing pictures and "making bumper stickers." He wanted to study the

Bible. Even as our friend accepted his son's negative feelings, he also recognized the desire for genuine Bible study. He was able to share this with the Sunday School leaders, and as a result the teachers began expecting much more from this class and challenged the students to serious study.

Beyond negative feelings, parents also will discover the good things happening in Sunday School. In talking with their children, parents should try to discover what they do like. They can discuss the many benefits of studying God's Word, together with good friends, taught by loving teachers. And parents can point out that in addition to helping us understand how God worked in the past, Sunday School lessons help us to understand God's eternal principles working in our lives today.

OBSERVE WHAT IS HAPPENING
IN CLASS ACTIVITIES

Teachers appreciate parents who express interest. As recent teachers of two sixth grade Sunday School classes, Elaine and I know how little contact parents sometimes have with teachers. So it's encouraging when parents do show concern for their children's educational experiences at church.

Parents can offer to help out—planning a social, providing transportation, or assisting with other class activities. Teachers always appreciate parents who are willing to open their home for a cookout or other informal activity. Once, when our youngest son was in high school, he informed us that his Sunday School friends had chosen our home (with stereo VCR) as the place to watch a video cassette of a Christian concert. We were pleased that they felt the freedom to do this and happy to support our son and his class. This kind of informal activity outside of class is very valuable and helps to enhance both interpersonal relationships and the quality of teaching in class.

Parents also can offer to help in the actual class time—perhaps substituting on a Sunday when the teacher must be absent. Sharing a hobby or vocation could supplement a unit of study. Observing and/or assisting a teacher are excellent ways to support the Sunday School. And the Sunday School students will be richer for it.

However, there is one caution. Becoming involved is not for "spying," but to make a meaningful contribution. This may be accomplished directly through specific participation, or indirectly through support that grows out of understanding.

One of our sons was a member of a very enthusiastic junior high department in our Sunday School. The teens were good kids but often got "carried away," and the superintendent was having trouble maintaining control. One set of parents agreed to sit in on the opening time to help maintain order. The dynamics of the group improved dramatically, and those parents were able to help the rest of us better understand and support the program.

Involved parents who recognize the needs in a

given class do well to remember the importance of consistent, informed prayer. Teaching God's Word with good application is a formidable task. A teacher who knows that the parents are praying regularly feels greatly encouraged. Such support could make the difference between "just making it" and succeeding gloriously.

SUPPORT SUNDAY SCHOOL AT HOME

Teachers can help parents model Sunday School support. If parents have negative, critical attitudes, their children will feel the same way. But even if parents aren't openly negative about Sunday School, ignoring it can be almost as harmful because parents usually support and promote those things they value. Here are some ideas we have used to support and promote this valuable resource. As teachers, we should share these with our students' parents.

1. Know what is going on in class. Review Sunday School materials that young children bring home—things like handcrafts, story reminders, and memory work. Ask the children about each one—what they learned as they made or used it, and what it means to them. Be sure to listen a lot and talk little.

When one of our sons was a preschooler, he proudly displayed a picture that he had drawn in Sunday School. Instead of listening, I tried to guess what it was. After I made several erroneous guesses, our son stalked off in disgust. It would have been far better if I had let him take the lead in explaining, rather than trying to control the conversation.

2. Read aloud the Bible and application stories from take-home papers. Discuss how they relate to the lessons learned. Use follow-up games or projects from the papers to reinforce the lesson and build family unity, too. We found it best to collect the take-home papers from our preschool children on the way home from church. Then we could be sure to use them sometime during the week. Since we had trouble with consistency anyway, this greatly minimized the slippage that tended to occur.

3. Take advantage of "home-use" elements built into curriculum materials. Look for helpful features in adult and children's lesson materials that can be done by the family. Ask children's teachers for suggestions to help plan family activities that build on and support Sunday School instruction.

Some publishers design their materials so that all ages study the same passage or a similar topic on a given Sunday. If you are using such materials, try to take advantage of this feature.

Other publishers offer different passages for each department so that any given age group will study a passage directly related to its needs. If a family has only one child, build that topic into home study. If there are children in more than one department, take advantage of the variety to enrich and broaden family understanding. Discuss topics from one child's materials on one day, and those from another child's on a different day.

4. Find out what passages, Bible stories, or topics will be taught in class and then read or study them throughout the week. By spending family time together in preparation and follow-up, parents can reinforce the impact of Sunday School. Use Bible story books or Bible resource books for further assistance.

Friends of ours had a daughter in a junior high Sunday School class studying biblical sexuality. They took the list of weekly topics and discussed the current one at the dinner table. This discussion enabled them to follow up on that topic and also gave them opportunity to review and to reinforce what their older children understood.

BECOME ACTIVELY INVOLVED

In the final analysis, the key to a good Sunday School program is committed teachers ministering in a well-designed, well-organized program. Most parents seem to agree that they should provide such a program for children. But who is "they?" According to God's Word, *parents* are the "they" who should be ministering to their children.

Some adults may have no children in the classes where help is most needed. All the more reason to help out. We should view the others in our church as part of our extended family. Just as our sons' aunts and uncles have contributed to their growth and maturity, our extended church family has contributed to our sons' spiritual growth and maturity.

Staffing continues to be a great problem for

Sunday School superintendents. Consequently, many classes are too large for effective teaching. But a superintendent cannot sub-divide classes unless Christians are willing to teach. And this is where parents come in. Some may become teachers. Or maybe it isn't teachers who are needed, but assistants to help with administrative functions. By shouldering that burden, parents can free a teacher to concentrate on instruction. And many parents find that being present during class time does wonders for the amount that their children learn. As teachers, we should not be afraid to encourage this kind of support.

THE RESULTS OF COOPERATION

All of these suggestions share a common theme—support! It's easy to ignore a program when we are not directly involved. Some of us may have complained, or (worse yet) undercut the ministry. But failing to support Sunday School can be devastating to our children. And those children are the future of our homes and churches.

Elaine and I, as parents, know that the Sunday School has been a vital resource in guiding our children to maturity, helping our sons to grow in loving God and other Christians, too. By the time our boys reached high school, they were looking for ways to minister to others. They have counseled in summer camps, served in the nursery, helped in VBS and Sunday School, and actively worked at telling unsaved friends and teammates about Christ. They have shared in various ministries through college including missions trips and Campus Life clubs.

But we alone cannot take the credit for what our sons are in the process of becoming. Whatever level of spiritual maturity they possess has been cultivated by many dedicated, godly adults who have taught them over the years. And many of those teachers continue to communicate love and support for our sons—even though their "teaching job" is long since finished.

Every one of us, as teachers and parents, can play this kind of vital role in ministering to children and young people. Naturally, such a commitment may cost us—but our children are worth it. And this is an investment that will pay handsome dividends. Perhaps your own children, or ones you teach, will respond to your involvement and become effective servants of God. And the church will continue to grow and mature as children, youth, and adults learn about God and serve Him.

Let's not let them down; we all need the Sunday School!

CONSIDER GOD'S WORD

There are many narrative portions in the Bible that *illustrate* how God's Word was taught or not taught. Yet, there are not very many specific passages that *instruct* us in the process of education. One of these instructive passages is Deuteronomy 6.

Read ***Deuteronomy 6:1-12.*** Notice that these verses talk about teaching God's Word to the next generation. Obviously, the primary application is to parents. But all adult Christians need to be concerned about the coming generations. These principles apply to all Christians, not just to parents.

Deuteronomy 6:1-3. These instructions were given to the Israelites as they were preparing to enter the Promised Land forty years after their first failure to occupy it. God reminded the leaders (verse 1) of the importance of knowing God's Word and obeying it.

> *Verse 2.* What was one consequence that God stated would result from fearing God and keeping His commandments?

> *Verse 3.* What was the other consequence that God said would result from obeying Him?

Deuteronomy 6:4-6. These verses speak to three aspects of spiritual commitment on the part of the teachers. The first aspect of spiritual living is knowing the truth (verse 4). We often stress

119

knowledge in our churches. Unfortunately, we may neglect the other two aspects—will and actions.

Verse 5. This verse speaks to our willful choice. How does God say we are to love Him?

Why do you think He stated it so forcefully?

Verse 6. In this verse, God explained the importance of doing what is right—having God's Word in our heart. Why do you think that many people who know what is right fail to live as God desires? You might want to compare Proverbs 3:5-6.

Deuteronomy 6:7-9 explains the process of teaching others so that they know and do what is right. The three techniques are *talking* (verse 7), *demonstrating* (verse 8), and *teaching* through a godly atmosphere (verse 9).

Deuteronomy 6:7. The first way in which we teach is by verbal communication. Verbal communication can take place anytime—it can be planned or spontaneous ("...when thou sittest in thine house, and when thou walkest by the way..."). What are some of the times that we can talk about God's Word spontaneously with our students and with our family?

What are some advantages of informal discussion compared to formal teaching time?

The second aspect of verbal communication is that it should be regular or systematic ("...when thou liest down, and when thou risest up..."). What are some times that parents or teachers can systematically talk about God's Word?

What are some benefits of systematic, regular, verbal communication?

Deuteronomy 6:8. In addition to talking about the Bible, we are to *show* Bible truth in action. When God told the Israelites to have His Word on their hands and foreheads, they took it literally. He also could have been giving them an object lesson—that their actions (on their hands) and their thoughts (on their foreheads) were to be controlled by God's Word. How can we teach God's Word to our children and students by our actions?

How will it be evident to others if our thoughts are controlled by the Word of God?

What effect will it have on children if adults (teachers or parents!) say one thing but do something else?

Deuteronomy 6:9. The third way to teach is by the very atmosphere of the home. Again the Jews took this literally, but this verse also could be a poetic expression—as soon as one walks into the yard or the home, it should be evident that the people in that home obey God. What specific things contribute to a godly atmosphere in a home that will help to teach God's Word to children?

What can parents do to enhance the educational value of the home's atmosphere?

Deuteronomy 6:10-12. This section ends with a caution. What warning did God give to the Israelites?

How does this warning apply to us in our country today?

CONSIDER YOUR MINISTRY

1. Verbal instruction for your students or children is a vital part of teaching God's Word. Do you talk about the Word spontaneously? When?

How could you structure more opportunities for informal, spontaneous discussion?

Do you talk about the Bible systematically? When?

What could you do to make such discussion more fruitful?

2. It is important for teachers to show the truth as well as talk about it. When do you have opportunities to demonstrate God's Word in action with your students?

What could you plan to do together with your students to give them more opportunity to see God's Word acted out in *your* life?

How do you think your students would respond to such activities?

3. The atmosphere of the home and classroom are important in spiritual teaching. What contributes to or enhances the instructive atmosphere in your classroom?

What could you do to improve your classroom atmosphere?

What can you do to include parents in your classroom or teaching?

How do you think such changes would influence what happens before, during, and after the lesson time?

8

A Parable for
Christian Travelers

"The weekly meeting of the Fellowship Travel Society will now come to order. Please let us stand and recite...."

Feeling depressed, with a sigh of resignation, I brace myself for another travel lecture—just like every other week. I feel worse than usual because Kiddie Cruiser Club hasn't gone very well this morning. Of course that shouldn't make much difference because Cruiser Club *never* goes well. The only real question seems to be whether the children will be rowdy or *very* rowdy.

I suppose I shouldn't blame them. What youngster wants to sit there week after week hearing lectures from an adult travel guide? My wife and I (we help out as Cruiser Captains) have never even visited many of the places we lecture about. But we try our best to get the kids excited about the wonders of travel anyway.

It might help if we had some videotapes showing the areas we study. Or slides. Or overhead transparencies. Or even some postcards. We've heard that some of the travel resource companies even publish workbooks for children and idea resources for the Captains. But our travel leader suggested that we concentrate on our Travel Guide. Cruiser Captains are free to teach whatever we want from the Guide. Maybe that's why the children we teach this year have "explored" the Amazon Rain Forest at least once in each of the last five years.

And then there's the Travel Guide itself. We adults sometimes struggle to understand it. It was written years and years ago—in another language I think—which may be why we need some help understanding it. To say nothing of what the children need. Sometimes we wonder if anything that we teach from the Guide sinks in.

Now don't get me wrong. I know that the Guide is reliable, and we really need to know what's in it. But the wife and I don't even know where to begin.

There's the history of travel, poems about travel, and exciting stories about great travelers of the past. But most of all, there are principles of travel—things we must know to help us get the most from our travel experience. And that's why we want our children to learn about travel. We've had such wonderful experiences that we want the same for our children.

But my wife and I don't think that we're communicating very well in Kiddie Cruiser Club. We suspect that most of the kids never pick up the Travel Guide between meetings. Many of them won't even bring their Guides to class. And they show more enthusiasm about some video game or TV show than about the incredible adventures of travel. But, then, that's about how most adults feel in the weekly TAMs. (That's short for Travel Adventure Meetings.) Their purpose (I think) is to help us learn about travel and to prepare ourselves for the adventures of travel—if any of us were ever to go anywhere.

Part of the problem is that our meetings are boring. I can tell you what's going to happen even before we leave home.

The Travel Leader will stand up and welcome us to the TAM, telling us what a wonderful meeting we are going to have. We'll all stand and recite our travel motto and then sing some travel songs. You know, songs like "On the Road to Mandalay," "Marching to Pretoria," and "Sentimental Journey." Then we'll pass the hat to help pay for some experts to establish Fellowship Travel Societies where there are none. Next comes the lecture. Our Travel Leader usually reads a section from the Travel Guide and then explains to us what it means. Once in a while our Leader will invite a guest travel expert to lecture us, and this provides some variety. But it sure is a long way from actually traveling somewhere.

The other day my wife and I were discussing our frustration with the Fellowship Travel Society. Of course Kiddie Cruiser Club is part of the problem, but we suspect that the real problem goes far deeper. We fondly recalled how it used to be when we first started the FTS. You knew we were charter members, didn't you?

It all began with several couples who used to go camping together. After a few times, we realized how much we could learn from each other and so we began getting together periodically to share our knowledge and expertise. From there it just grew. Campground and resort information, travel brochures, tapes, hours spent talking, dreaming, and planning our vacations. But the best part of all was the travel, actually experiencing the joy and adventure of the trip.

Finally, someone (we think it was George, but it could have been Ethel) came up with the idea of FTS—the Fellowship Travel Society. We could learn together about travel. We could study, share, and plan. Then all of us—whether in a group, as a family, or just individually—could get the most out of our travel experiences. So we began meeting weekly, and the FTS was born.

Before long we recognized that the children were not getting involved the way the adults were. Which is why we began the Kiddie Cruiser Club. We wanted our children to have experiences like ours but on their own level of understanding.

Unfortunately, the sad reality is that their experiences really are like ours—more so than we care to admit. They come because their parents tell them to, and the parents come because they feel that they ought to attend.

"...Ends our lecture for today. Please join us next week for an exciting action-packed lecture on the history of luggage entitled 'Be Glad You Aren't an Alligator.' And as you leave, remember to pick up our new brochure 'Tips for Hassle-free Packing.' You are dismissed."

* * * * *

Perhaps the parable of the Fellowship Travel Society will help us to examine our own attitudes and ministries. At one time or another all of us question just how effectively we are teaching Sunday School. But few people know what to do when the sense of frustration—the feeling that we are just going through the motions—overwhelms us.

If you feel that way, there is some good news for you. The problem may not be entirely you or your teaching. My experience with local churches suggests that even if you do need to sharpen some of your skills, you may be only part of the problem. Most churches suffer from "ministry fragmentation."

A church is characterized by fragmented ministry when individual programs have a life and/or purpose of their own apart from the overall purpose of the church. When this happens, competition and even conflict between programs can result.

The solution can be relatively simple, but it requires cooperation on the part of pastoral and lay staff in the church. With a little effort, and some strategic planning on their part, Sunday School teachers and other ministry leaders can have a sense of purpose and also a means to evaluate the effectiveness of what they are doing. A great way to deal with the fragmented ministry problem that you may be sensing is to ask four simple questions.

(Caution: Sometimes it takes quite a bit of work to come up with good answers.)

Why Does Our Church Exist? At first there seems to be a very simple answer. We exist to glorify God. But what about reaching the lost? And how about influencing society? Don't churches have a primary responsibility for providing encouragement and fellowship to believers?

All of those are good answers, but they are not the reason why your church exists—a ministry different from the one down the street. What makes your church unique? What would your town lose if your church were to close? What are the objectives of your church's ministry?

Every church needs to identify its own unique place in the kingdom of God. Often this is called a "mission statement," or "statement of purpose." Each individual in a given church should know why that particular church exists. But individual members cannot determine the answer. It must come from the pastors and lay leaders of the church.

If you don't have a ready answer for why your individual church exists, then talk to your leaders. Probably, you will find that sometime in the past the leaders of your church formulated such a statement. Ask them to dig it out of the closet, dust it off, and examine it closely. Everyone may be surprised at how good it is. Over the years people often forget why their church was started. When this happens, empty routine and unevaluated repetition may proliferate.

Perhaps the purpose statement needs some updating. Your community may have changed; there may be new or different needs. While the

Great Commission remains the same, the way *your* church expresses it may have changed somewhat. The time spent evaluating, and modifying if necessary, your purpose statement will breathe new life into your church, It can add enthusiasm and dynamism to a routine, business-as-usual approach to ministry.

What Primary Needs Are We Addressing? This second question follows a reaffirmation of your purpose statement. Obviously, no church can meet every one of society's potential needs. Some churches strongly emphasize evangelism while others concentrate on education. Foreign missions is a high priority in another church. One church may have a counseling center, while another addresses the need for preschool education and day care or ministry to the deaf or handicapped.

To identify the primary needs that a church meets, list all of the potential needs that *could* be addressed. You may discover scores of needs crying for ministry. Once you have compiled your list, take your purpose statement and identify those needs that relate to *your* basic purpose. Usually this generates a manageable list of ministry needs which your church can address that in turn can be grouped into several categories.

For example, a church might recognize that several needs can be categorized as evangelistic—reaching the lost. Another group of needs might focus on education, while a third group could include ministering physically to those in need.

After you have completed this task, you are

ready to ask a third question.

What Needs Does My Program Meet?
Ordinarily a church program should address a specific set of needs.

For example, if you teach in the Sunday School you may recognize that the primary focus of your program is the educational needs of those who attend your church. Another church, with a strong outreach program, may make evangelism the primary focus for its Sunday School.

Which of these is valid?

Probably either one depending on what a church decides to emphasize. But if you don't know your church's focus, as a Sunday School teacher you could become frustrated.

One teacher came to me in great agitation. *Her* purpose in Sunday School was to provide in-depth education for Christian kids. But her church had an extensive bus ministry. Consequently, many students were totally unchurched and unfamiliar with church. As we talked, she realized that her church's Sunday School program was designed primarily for evangelism. When she understood the conflict, she was able to modify her approach in order to succeed in her unique Sunday School.

This leads to the fourth, and final, question.

How Can I Minister Effectively In My Program? Working to achieve the objectives of your particular program is a good start. But effective ministry goes beyond that.

Once you know your goals, materials and

methods become important. The content of what you teach and the resources you use should reflect your program objectives.

Of course, your leaders need to provide good materials to help you do your job. When leaders fail to provide adequate materials, it is often out of ignorance not malice. They don't intend to cause frustration, but staff leaders may not realize what their teachers need. It is your responsibility to communicate your classroom needs clearly and specifically. Let your leader know what problems you have encountered. Together you may discover resources that will enhance and contribute to your effective teaching.

Once you have good materials and a sense of direction, your regular preparation becomes enjoyable. Often, in-class discipline problems arise out of using the wrong materials or from lack of teacher preparation. If you don't come to class with a clear understanding of what you want to accomplish and how you are going to do it, the students may well substitute *their* "objectives" for yours. And once they are in control, get set for a long and noisy session.

But if you go into your classroom well-prepared, with a good lesson plan, everyone will be far happier. And you will be well on your way to an effective ministry that helps to fulfill the purpose of your church.

Whether you participate in a travel society or a church, being part of an organization that was once dynamic and exciting, but has lost its reason for existence, is a terrible experience. Routine replaces purposeful action, and indifference leads to boredom. Participation grows out of a sense of obligation rather than anticipation that something meaningful is taking place.

Jesus condemned the Pharisees because they went through the motions of spiritual activity, missing the true purpose of what they were doing (Matthew 23:1-36). We need to cultivate good spiritual habits, but church ministry must go beyond habit. It must be involvement that not only gives us something to do several times a week, but also equips us for the greatest adventure of all. The adventure of living the Christian life is not for armchair Christians, just hearing someone else tell us about it.

CONSIDER GOD'S WORD

It may not always be appropriate, but we tend to place more emphasis on what a person says near the end of life than what was said earlier. Why? Perhaps because as one approaches the end of life, he or she is forced to think about the realities of eternity. At this time, we assume that a person will share those things they found most important.

When a leader is leaving a group of followers, ordinarily that person communicates concepts that are important to the continuing effectiveness of that group. Jesus did as He neared the end of His time on earth. He called the eleven remaining disciples to Him and gave them final instructions. We call these final words the Great Commission.

None of the Gospels includes all of the events near the end of Christ's life, but Matthew summarizes this part of Jesus' instructions. In this commission, Jesus assigned certain tasks to His followers and gave them certain promises.

Matthew 28:16-20. As you read these verses, try to picture the scene in your mind. Jesus is meeting with His disciples on a mountain in Galilee. It was a remote place. Some of them are still reeling in confusion and pain from the events of the preceding days. A few still struggle with questions over what really happened (verse 17). It is likely that there was much more conversation than Matthew recorded, but his summary gives us all the details we need. Jesus assured His followers that He was in charge. He gave them their assignment, and He promised help and support.

Matthew 28:18. The word "power" could be translated "authority." Why is it important to know that Jesus has all authority?

What is the extent of this authority?

Who granted Him this authority?

Matthew 28:19-20. The notes in the *Ryrie Study Bible* on these verses are helpful. In Greek, there is one command in these two verses, "teach all nations" (literally, "make disciples of all nations"). Three subordinate verbs describe what it means to make disciples: "going" ("Go ye," verse 19), "baptizing" (verse 19), and "teaching" (verse 20).

The basic command in these verses is to "make disciples." How did early Christians fulfill this command?

What difference did it make in the first century and what difference should it make to you now?

Matthew 28:19-20a. There are three subordinate words (participles in Greek) that describe the action of making disciples (followers of Jesus).

> *Going* is a general word without any specific statements as to where Jesus' followers were to go. Why do you think that Jesus was not more specific in giving His disciples designated geographical assignments?

The second word describing making disciples is "baptizing." Although Jesus certainly meant baptism as we think of it, it probably included even more than many realize today.

In the first century, when a person was baptized, it was a public commitment to becoming a follower of Christ. Similar to "going forward" when we accept Christ today, physical baptism was the logical, public expression of that commitment.

> What were some of the obstacles that first century individuals faced in deciding to follow Jesus?

The third descriptive word is "teaching." What

UNLEASHING THE TEACHER IN YOU!

was it that Jesus instructed His disciples to teach?

How well do you think they did it?

Matthew 28:20b. Notice how this passage ends. Jesus did not leave His followers on their own to fulfill His command. What promise could His followers count on?

What difference would this have made in their attitudes toward the task?

John 14:3-4,16-20. Although Jesus was about to leave the earth after commissioning His followers, the verses from John 14 should have been a great encouragement to them. How could Jesus be with His followers even though He was leaving?

How do you think they felt about His promises? (How would *you* have felt?)

CONSIDER YOUR MINISTRY

1. How does your church contribute to fulfilling the three aspects of the Great Commission (to make disciples)?

Going —

Baptizing —

Teaching —

141

2. Think about your own ministry. Which aspect(s) of the Great Commission does your ministry emphasize?

How does this contribute to the church's overall goal of making disciples?

Are there aspects of the program in which you minister that could be changed to make it more effective?

3. Think about your own personal involvement in ministry. How do you personally contribute to fulfilling the Great Commission?

Going —

Baptizing (leading people to Christ) —

Teaching —

4. How does the promise of Christ's continual ministry to you through the person of the Holy Spirit make a difference in the way you approach your ministry?

9

How to Kill a Sunday School

Many American Sunday Schools are not healthy. Most struggle to maintain their enrollment and to staff their classes. As I speak with leaders across our country, the number one question pastors and local church educators ask is, "How can we staff our Sunday Schools?"

In a recent meeting of local church Christian educators, we were discussing the problems of recruiting workers for their Sunday Schools. One leader explained that in the past he recruited teachers to serve indefinitely, but now he asks for only a one-year commitment. Another related that he had given up on yearly recruiting and was trying to get teachers to commit to one quarter at a time. A third leader ruefully reported that he had given up quarterly recruiting. He was trying to get teachers to commit to a month, but was considering lowering his request to one week at a time.

Although most churches continue to emphasize Sunday School as their key Christian education program, those who attend church seem to value it differently.

According to the *Yearbook of American and*

Canadian Churches (Abingdon Press, 1970 and 1990), the 1970 total reported enrollment in American Sunday Schools was 40.5 million students. By the 1990 report, enrollment had dropped to about 25 million. This is not a good sign.

At one time many evangelical churches had Sunday School attendances that equalled or exceeded worship attendance. But the proportion has changed. Informal surveys I have taken in recent years indicate that in many churches Sunday School attendance has dropped to about two-thirds (or less) of the morning worship attendance.

Sunday Schools are not healthy. If the same number drop out in the twenty years after 1990 as they did in the twenty years before 1990, twenty years from now, national Sunday School attendance will drop to about 10 million—one-fourth of what it was in 1970.

But many seem to be ignoring the problems, hoping they will go away. Of course, they may be right. If we ignore Sunday School problems, they very well may go away. And then we will have no more Sunday Schools to worry about. Indeed, some seem to act as though they would be happy to be rid of Sunday School—the agency that has been called the most significant lay ministry in the history of Christianity. Historian C.B. Eavey wrote about Sunday School, "So great has been its contribution to the world that it has been called the University of the People" (*History of Christian Education*).

While studying the history of the Sunday School, I discovered five key elements that contributed to the success of American Sunday Schools.

1) Sunday Schools were operated as an integral part of church programming.

2) They were recognized as a supplementary resource to assist parents in their task of Christian education.

3) Effective Sunday Schools included adults as well as children.

4) The basic Sunday School adopted a wide variety of forms to meet unique needs in given churches.

5) Sunday School transcended social class and denominational distinctives (Willis, *200 Years and Still Counting*).

But in spite of the brilliant history and great potential for the future, many with historical tunnel vision and ministry myopia seem determined to eliminate the Sunday School. So for their benefit, let's consider four simple steps that will help us put it to rest gently and swiftly.

STRATEGY ONE: Ignore the needs of Sunday School students.

What we really need to do is just run the program. Forget about the needs of people. It requires time and effort to evaluate people's needs and then to design an effective ministry that will meet those needs. We all know what Sunday School is. After all, didn't we attend as children? Those were the good old days, and we ought to have the kind of programs that we had then. Let's run Sunday School the way it's always been run.

But there is a better way. Most people forget that the original Sunday Schools were established to teach illiterate children to read and to write so that they could read the Bible and worship intelligently. The first schools ran for about seven hours each Sunday, and some of the teachers were paid. Because those Sunday Schools met people's needs, they grew, rapidly spreading around the world. But in each geographical region, Sunday School assumed a unique form based on local needs. Sunday Schools were never "one program." They were countless programs. Each one was unique—adapted to the context where it operated.

STRATEGY TWO: Assume that people will attend.

After all, if we offer the program, we've done our job, haven't we? Why should we worry about pastoral support for the program? Just because no other local church programs succeed without pastoral attention and promotion doesn't mean we need it. Why confuse our people with statements of objectives for Sunday School? And there shouldn't be any need to generate enthusiasm through promotion and publicity. Those things take an awful lot of work. And they might even cost some money, too.

But there is a better way. Successful Sunday Schools are exciting places to be. A high level of enthusiasm and expectation characterizes them. People share what is happening—how God is working. And usually there are very clear statements of why people should attend and what benefit they will receive. Leaders *and* students understand how the Sunday School complements other ministries of the church. Members know they will feel the loss if they miss one week. Some even choose not to go to the cottage every summer weekend because they value meaningful Bible study and quality Christian fellowship.

STRATEGY THREE: Accept any who are willing to teach.

After all, if we demand too much from our teachers, they might not show up. And we are desperate. We need to twist arms and recruit people even if they are immature Christians, know nothing about teaching, and are too busy to follow through on a commitment. Forget job descriptions, standards, and faithfulness. If they've been in the church for a few years, they probably don't even need to study. If they just show up in the classroom by the time class is supposed to begin (or as soon after that as convenient), they'll be okay.

But there is a better way. Growing, thriving Sunday Schools make high demands on their teachers. Wise leaders expect teachers to study and to prepare for their classes. The teachers are encouraged (or required) to visit and spend time with students outside of class. Arriving late is anathema—teachers need to arrive in class early, ready to greet the first students when they arrive. In effective Sunday Schools, teaching is a top priority. If the demands of other good ministries conflict with Sunday School teaching and preparation, then teachers have to decide which they want to do—either teach in Sunday School or work in another ministry.

STRATEGY FOUR: Don't bother to provide any resources for your Sunday School teachers.

Let them teach whatever they want. After all, they are the ones doing the teaching, aren't they? They can just read the Bible. And if teachers need supplementary resources or equipment, let them buy those with their own money. Times are tough and the church budget is stretched already.

But there is a better way. Where Sunday Schools are effective, the Bible is taught with quality materials carefully chosen to help accomplish the goals for the Sunday School ministry. Instead of every teacher doing his or her own thing, there is a scope and sequence that avoids both gaps and overlap. It provides a balance between content and application. The facilities are clean, bright, and cheerful. Church leaders make sure that needed resources and equipment are readily available.

Sunday School has been a powerful influence in the lives and ministries of Christians for over two hundred years. And in countless churches throughout the world it continues as an effective program of Christian education. But we can't assume that it will continue as such without attention and effort. Wherever a Sunday School languishes, there are obvious reasons for its failure. But a Sunday School with clearly defined goals, carefully coordinated with other church ministries, staffed by properly recruited and trained teachers, equipped with quality facilities and curriculum materials can transform your church and community.

On the other hand, if you choose to ignore the problems of Sunday School, it probably will go away.

But what about those churches where leaders have developed an alternative to Sunday School? Obviously it is possible to provide Christian education without a Sunday School. But what I find happening in many churches is that the leaders have not designed an effective program to replace Sunday School. What ordinarily happens when Sunday School languishes and declines is that leaders discontinue the program with no real alternative. And so whatever Christian education was going on ceases completely.

It is possible to have Christian education without Sunday School. But it will not happen by accident. If we are to have good educational programs, we need to plan them intentionally. Whether we call these programs Sunday School or some other name, effective ministries must follow biblical guidelines.

Christ commanded His followers to "make disciples of all the nations" (NASB). Such disciple-making was to be done by going, baptizing, and teaching persons to practice everything that Jesus commanded (Matthew 28:19-20). A legitimate Christian education program must reflect the biblical principles of passages such as Matthew 28:19-20; II Timothy 1:10-11, 2:2, 3:16-17;

Ephesians 4:11-16; Luke 6:40, and many others. Several qualities mark any effective Christian education program.

Quality Relationships with Students. A truly effective ministry needs to build on excellent teacher/student relationships. Jesus preached to many, but the focus of His ministry was to a few, in depth.

Instruction in Bible Content. Jesus did more than just love His disciples. He communicated God's truth to them. Christian education demands that students know what God has revealed. Jesus explained that one of the ministries of the Holy Spirit is to "...bring to your remembrance all that I said to you" (John 14:26, NASB).

Application to Life. While there must be a factual, content emphasis, we also need to teach Bible truth in the context of life. James explained that if we are teaching our students a kind of faith that doesn't result in godly behavior, it is not real faith. Biblical Christianity makes a difference in how we live. It produces purity of life and ministry to others (James 1:25-27).

Any valid Sunday School program will include these elements. But what about other programs which accomplish similar purposes? May they increase and thrive. We should not limit ourselves to only one ministry. Weekday ministries such as Christian Service Brigade, Pioneer Clubs, Awana,

CEF, small group fellowships, youth para-church ministries, Nav 2:7, local church hybrid programs, and countless others include such elements.

Perhaps the most exciting trend that I have observed in recent years is the emphasis on small groups. From coast to coast, believers are meeting in small groups for Bible study, fellowship, mutual support, and caring. Most healthy churches that I've seen have a strong network of small groups. Generally, they have strong Sunday Schools, too.

We can have CE programs *without* Sunday School, and we can achieve excellent CE *through* it. But, we need to make sure that each of our programs is excellent, reflecting biblical guidelines.

With quality programs, we can lead individuals to a commitment to accept Jesus Christ as their Savior. And we can help them grow through Bible study. Then, if we really are doing our job, they will mature to where they will move into significant positions of ministry. And the whole church will continue to grow and mature "...joined and held together by every supporting ligament, grows and builds itself up in love, as each part does its work" (Ephesians 4:16, NIV).

CONSIDER GOD'S WORD

Books on teaching can easily give the impression that if a teacher does the right things, quality education is guaranteed. Perhaps some have felt that this book implied such a promise. If so, then we have done an injustice to teachers everywhere.

No matter how hard a teacher works or how well that teacher prepares, students may choose not to learn. In fact, one of Jesus' best-known parables deals with this very topic. The Parable of the Sower teaches, among other things, that the condition of the one who is taught plays a major role in whether or not that individual receives the Word of God.

Read *Matthew 13:3-9, 18-23.* Some have renamed this the Parable of the Soils instead of the Sower because Jesus so emphasized the condition of the soil in receiving the good seed. Notice in the interpretation of the parable (verses 18-23), the seed is God's Word; the sower is one who distributes the Word, and the various soils are the hearts of those who receive the Word. Regardless of what the sower does, the condition of the heart and other circumstances are the primary influence on the effectiveness of the Word.

Matthew 13:4,19. The fields in Jesus' day were often crisscrossed with footpaths. Wherever people walked, the ground was packed hard. If seed fell on this ground, the birds would eat it. What kind of heart is represented by the hard ground?

Who are some people whose hearts are hardened like the packed soil?

Why does Satan want to "snatch up the Word" of God?

Matthew 13:5-6,20-21. In many places throughout Palestine, the soil is rocky, or large rocks lay just a few inches below the surface. What kind of heart is the rocky soil?

What happened to these seeds after they sprouted?

Identify some people who appeared to follow God's Word, but fell away when the "going" (discipleship) got difficult.

Matthew 13:7,22. All good gardeners know the importance of weeding a garden. What kind of heart is represented by the soil where the seeds got choked?

The problem did not seem to be with the soil but with the weeds that sprouted and grew in that soil. What chokes out God's Word in people's lives?

What concerns in your life might crowd out God's Word?

Matthew 13:8,23. What was the result of sowing the seed on good soil?

What fruit is produced when a person receives the Word and applies it to his life?

155

What does the varying amount of production (hundredfold, sixtyfold, thirtyfold) indicate about response to the Bible and about ministry?

CONSIDER YOUR MINISTRY

Although we may minister to people who are like any of the four soils, we who teach should recognize ourselves in the fourth soil. The very fact that one has responded to the Word and is involved in ministry indicates that person probably is the productive soil. Of course, not all soil, even productive soil, produces the same amount. In God's sovereign wisdom, we each produce our own amount of fruit. It is He who gives the increase.

As soon as one belongs to the fourth category, the productive soil, that person also becomes a sower. Perhaps that is why Jesus called this the Parable of the Sower (Matthew 13:18).

And as any good farmer knows, preparation of the ground to receive the seed is critical. A farmer who plants seed with no soil preparation should not expect a good harvest.

So we, as sowers of the Word, need to be concerned with preparing the hearts of our students.

Consider how we may do this.

1. Often a heart becomes hard due to circumstances. Do any of your students seem to have hardened hearts? Who?

What circumstances do you think created such a condition?

How can you show love and concern for that individual to help soften his or her heart?

2. We often find shallow students in our classes. They seem to grow and mature for awhile, but their interest and enthusiasm decline very quickly. Which of your students may have shown growth spurts but are disinterested now?

What contributed to such a decline in interest?

If you don't know, can you find out?

How can you make contact with these students to try and draw them back to renewed growth?

How do you think they will respond?

3. Even students who are growing and maturing are influenced by life's cares and concerns. Perhaps family problems or needs and pressures have overwhelmed some. Others may be caught up in materialism or other overpowering desires. Which of your students might be in this category?

How can you demonstrate a proper value system for them?

What class activities or projects could help class members put their situations into perspective?

4. Since you, the teacher, are the sower, what are you doing to help prepare the soil of your students' hearts to receive the seed of God's Word?

What personal factors might make the difference between a student who bears fruit thirtyfold and one who bears fruit a hundredfold?

Do you see spiritual productivity in your students' lives? Who is growing? Who is not growing?

What strategies could help increase the spiritual fruitfulness of your students?

<u>Student</u>   <u>Strategy</u>